IF I SHOULD DIE

BOSTON UNIVERSITY STUDIES IN PHILOSOPHY AND RELIGION

General Editor: Leroy S. Rouner

Volume Twenty-Two

If I Should Die

Edited by

Leroy S. Rouner

UNIVERSITY OF NOTRE DAME PRESS
Notre Dame, Indiana

Manufactured in the United States of America

Library of Congress Cataloging-in-Publication Data

If I should die / edited by Leroy S. Rouner.
    p.   cm. — (Boston University studies in philosophy and
religion ; vol. 22)
    Includes bibliographical references and index.
    ISBN 0-268-03160-6 (cloth : alk. paper)
    ISBN 0-268-03161-4 (paper : alk. paper)
    1. Death—Religious aspects.   2. Immortality (Philosophy).
I. Rouner, Leroy S.   II. Series.
    BL504.I3   2001
    291.2'3—dc21   00-011593

FOR RITA RAINSFORD ROUNER

Philosopher of grief and loss; Theologian of God's surprises; Poet of the inarticulate heart's tone; her Institute lecture and her poems showed us a way from desolation to hope, because some bonds are forever.

Contents

PART III: THE PHILOSOPHY OF LIFE AND
THE PROBLEM OF IMMORTALITY

Preface

Boston University Studies in Philosophy and Religion is a joint project of the Boston University Institute for Philosophy and Religion and the University of Notre Dame Press. The essays in each annual volume are edited from the previous year's lecture program and invited papers of the Boston University Institute. The Director of the Institute, who is also the General Editor of these Studies, chooses a theme and invites participants to lecture at Boston University in the course of the academic year. The Editor then selects and edits the essays to be included in the volume. Dr. Barbara Darling-Smith, Assistant Director of the Institute, regularly copy-edits the essays. In preparation is Volume 23, *Courage*.

The Boston University Institute for Philosophy and Religion was begun informally in 1970 under the leadership of Professor Peter Bertocci of the Department of Philosophy, with the cooperation of Dean Walter Muelder of the School of Theology, Professor James Purvis, Chair of the Department of Religion, and Professor Marx Wartofsky, Chair of the Department of Philosophy. Professor Bertocci was concerned to institutionalize one of the most creative features of Boston personalism, its interdisciplinary approach to fundamental issues of human life. When Professor Leroy S. Rouner became Director in 1975, and the Institute became a formal part of the Boston University Graduate School, every effort was made to continue that vision of an ecumenical and interdisciplinary forum.

Within the University the Institute is committed to open interchange on fundamental issues in philosophy and religious study which transcend the narrow specializations of academic curricula. We seek to counter those trends in higher education which emphasize technical expertise in a "multi-versity" and gradually transform undergraduate liberal arts education into preprofessional training.

Our programs are open to the general public and are often broadcast on WBUR-FM, Boston University's National Public Radio station. Outside the University we seek to recover the public tradition of philosophical discourse which was a lively part of American intellectual life in the early years of this century before the professionalization of both philosophy and religious reflection made these two disciplines virtually unavailable even to an educated public. We note, for example, that much of William James's work was presented originally as public lectures, and we are grateful to James's present-day successors for the significant public papers which we have been honored to publish. This commitment to a public tradition in American intellectual life has important stylistic implications. At a time when too much academic writing is incomprehensible, or irrelevant, or both, our goal is to present readable essays by acknowledged authorities on critical human issues.

Acknowledgments

Barbara Darling-Smith, Assistant Director of the Institute, continues to be the person who makes our program work. During the year she runs the office, greets guests, instructs our work-study students, contacts lecturer/authors, rides herd on the budget, and does other graceful and kindly things which have never made their way into a job description. During the late spring and early summer—in addition to all this—she does manuscript preparation for our annual volume. This is not simply copy-editing; it is also gentle nudging of schedule-impaired authors, genial negotiations with our friend Ann Rice at Notre Dame Press about publication dates, and some dark and definitive deliberations which are best kept in-house. Barbara is now leaving her responsibilities as Assistant Director to Anna Lännström, but she happily continues with the Institute as Managing Editor of this series.

We would not have a book were it not for the generosity of our authors. Those outside Boston University are not adequately paid, and my Boston University colleagues are not paid at all, so there is no good economic reason why this venture should work. But the old Liberal argument that everything finally comes down to economics is given the lie by these gracious participants in a venture which holds little reward except the satisfaction of knowing that they have made a careful public statement on an important issue about which they cared deeply. So once again we have occasion to thank them for their generosity and their fine work.

Contributors

WENDY DONIGER first trained as a dancer under George Balanchine and Martha Graham, and then went on to graduate *summa cum laude* from Radcliffe College and complete two doctorates in Sanskrit and Indian Studies from Harvard and Oxford. She has taught at Harvard, Oxford, the University of London, and the University of California at Berkeley and is at present the Mircea Eliade Professor of the History of Religions at the University of Chicago. A much-honored scholar and a prolific writer, she has been President of the American Academy of Religion, and is a Fellow of the American Academy of Arts and Sciences. Her writings range from translations of Sanskrit poems and Hindu myths to books about hallucinogenic mushrooms, phallic worship, evil, karma, women, dreams, folklore, horses, and myths. She has also written over 150 articles and many reviews. Her works in progress include *The Mythology of Horses in India* and *The Bed Trick: Sex, Myth and Masquerade*.

MALCOLM DAVID ECKEL is Associate Professor of Religion and Associate Director of the Division of Religious and Theological Studies at Boston University. He has taught at Middlebury College and Harvard University, where he received his Ph.D. and later became administrative Director of the Center for the Study of World Religions. He has traveled widely in Southeast Asia and has specialized in Buddhist philosophy. He edited the selected essays of J. L. Mehta under the title *India and the West: The Problem of Understanding* and is the author of *Jñanagarbha's Commentary on the Distinction Between the Two Truths* and *To See the Buddha: A Philosopher's Quest for the Meaning of Emptiness*.

AARON V. GARRETT did his Ph.D. at the New School in New York, and is now Assistant Professor of Philosophy at Boston University. He has published a number of articles in the history of modern philosophy, particularly on Spinoza, Hobbes, and Hume, and a forthcoming article "Human Nature" in the *Cambridge History of Eighteenth-Century Philosophy*. His edited volumes include *Animal Rights and Animal Souls in the Eighteenth Century*, *Buffon's Natural History: General and Particular* and Lord Monboddo's *Ancient Metaphysics*. He is currently completing a book-length manuscript on Spinoza's method and a critical edition of Francis Hutcheson's *An Essay on the Nature and Conduct of the Passions and Affections, with Illustrations on the Moral Sense*.

PETER JOHN GOMES is Plummer Professor of Christian Morals and Pusey Minister in the Memorial Church at Harvard University. He was educated at Bates College and Harvard Divinity School and taught at the Tuskegee Institute in Alabama before coming to Harvard in 1970. He is the holder of nine honorary degrees, and has served on numerous Boards of Trustees, including those of Wellesley and Bates Colleges, the New England Conservatory of Music, the English Speaking Union, and the Pilgrim Society of Plymouth. He has been the Lyman Beecher Lecturer at Yale Divinity School, and participated in the Presidential Inauguration ceremonies for both Ronald Reagan and George Bush. He is the author of numerous papers, sermon collections, and public lectures but is perhaps best known for *The Good Book: Reading the Bible with Mind and Heart* and *Sermons: Biblical Wisdom for Daily Living*.

BRIAN W. JORGENSEN is Assistant Professor of Humanities and Assistant Professor of English at Boston University. He is also Assistant Dean in the College of Liberal Arts where he supervises the program of the Core Curriculum. His degrees are in English Literature from the University of Notre Dame (B.A.), and Northwestern University (M.A. and Ph.D.) His teaching ranges from ancient philosophy through classical literature and drama; Shakespeare, romantic and modern poetry, and modern philosophy, especially the work of Martin Heidegger and Alfred North Whitehead. At Boston University he has also served on the Board of the

Center for Ethics and Character at the School of Education, the Dean's Committee on the Revision of the College of Liberal Arts Divisional Studies Program, and the development committee for the College of Liberal Arts Honors Program.

JOHN LACHS studied at McGill University before doing his Ph.D. in Philosophy at Yale. He taught at the College of William and Mary from 1959 to 1966 and at present is the Centennial Professor of Philosophy at Vanderbilt University. He has won numerous teaching awards including the E. Harris Harbison Award for Distinguished Teaching in 1967, the Madison Sarratt Prize for Excellence in Undergraduate Teaching in 1972, and the Outstanding Commitment to Teaching Freshmen Award in 1999. He has written and edited a number of books on American philosophy, including several on George Santayana, and a forthcoming collection of essays on the philosophy of William Ernest Hocking. His own philosophy is spelled out in a number of books on the philosophy of life including *The Relevance of Philosophy to Life*, *In Love with Life*, and *The Cost of Comfort*.

JÜRGEN MOLTMANN is Professor of Systematic Theology *Emeritus* at the University of Tübingen, and he has also been Woodruff Visiting Professor at Emory University. His first degree, doctorate, and habilitation degree are all from the University of Göttingen. His 1967 *Theology of Hope* has become one of the most influential theological works of the post-World War II period. He is also well known for his theology of the cross developed in *The Crucified God* and for his articulations of political theology. His extensive bibliography also includes *The Church in the Power of the Spirit*, *The Future of Creation*, *Experiences of God*, *The Trinity and the Kingdom*, and *God in Creation*. Among his many honors are the Elba Literary Prize and the Gifford Lectureship.

DAVID L. ROOCHNIK is Associate Professor of Philosophy at Boston University, where he has won a number of distinguished teaching awards, most recently the Metcalf Award for Excellence in Teaching in May 1999. Prior to coming to Boston University he taught at Iowa State University and Williams College, among other places. His fields of specialization are ancient Greek philosophy and ancient Greek literature, and his books include *The Tragedy of Reason: Toward a Platonic Conception of Logos* and *Of Art and Wisdom: Plato's Understanding of Techne.* He is a graduate of Trinity College (B.A.) and Pennsylvania State University (M.A., Ph.D.).

LEROY S. ROUNER taught at the United Theological College, Bangalore, India (1961-1966), before becoming Professor of Philosophy, Religion, and Philosophical Theology and Director of the Institute for Philosophy and Religion at Boston University. He studied at Harvard College, Union Theological Seminary (New York), and Columbia University. He has edited nineteen volumes in the Boston University Studies in Philosophy and Religion series and contributed to many of them. He has also edited *Philosophy, Religion, and the Coming World Civilization: Essays in Honor of William Ernest Hocking.* He is the author of *Within Human Experience: The Philosophy of William Ernest Hocking; The Long Way Home* (a memoir); and *To Be at Home: Christianity, Civil Religion, and World Community.* He and Rita Rainsford Rouner recently celebrated their forty-fifth wedding anniversary.

RITA RAINSFORD ROUNER graduated from Smith College in 1948 and subsequently studied at Andover Newton Theological School and Union Theological Seminary in New York, where she completed an M. Div. Degree. She also holds the D.Min. degree from Boston University in Pastoral Counseling. From 1961 to 1966 she was a missionary in South India with her husband, and later was a Pastoral Counselor and Spiritual Director at the Episcopal Divinity School in Cambridge, Massachusetts, and in private practice. She comes from a family of preachers and poets. Her paternal grandfather, William S. Rainsford, was senior minister of St. George's Episcopal Church in New York City when J. P. Morgan was head of the vestry. Her father, Kerr Rainsford, was an architect who published two book-length epic poems, one on Harold of England and one on Joan of Arc. Her mother, Christina Nichols Rainsford, published four volumes of poems, and her great-aunt, Katrina Trask, was co-founder with her husband of Yaddo, the artists' colony in Saratoga, New York. Rita Rouner has published poems in *The American Scholar*, *Appalachia*, and *Climbing* magazine. Most of the poems in her essay appear for the first time in print. She is the mother of four children.

DAVID SCHMIDTZ is Professor of Philosophy and Joint Professor of Economics at the University of Arizona. He did his undergraduate work at the Universities of Calgary and Saskatchewan, and his Ph.D. is from the University of Arizona. He taught at Yale from 1988 to 1994 and spent a year at Bowling Green State University before moving to Arizona in 1995. He teaches ethics, social and political philosophy, as well as the philosophy of law, the philosophy of economics, and Decision Theory. His books include *The Limits of Government: An Essay on the Public Goods Argument*; *Rational Choice and Moral Agency*; *Social Welfare and Individual Responsibility* (with Robert E. Goodwin), and *Environmental Ethics: Introductory Readings* (with Elizabeth Willott). He is currently editing a *Festschrift* for Robert Nozick, and is a contributor to that volume.

Introduction

LEROY S. ROUNER

NOTHING IS MORE certain in life than death, and no period in history has suffered the pervasive presence of death more than this present generation. In America, however, neither our public nor our private philosophies have reflected this overwhelming fact. We have publicly debated issues like abortion and the death penalty, but the context has been human rights, or social justice, not the meaning of life and death. Privately we have mourned our personal losses—grandparents, parents, dear friends—but like obedient children who have been warned not to make a fuss, we usually keep our grief to ourselves. Our parents wore black for a year, and had funerals. Death stopped them in their tracks, at least for a time. We wear sport coats and print dresses and have "Celebrations of Life," as though death has no power to invade our daily round.

Very little has been written on the reality of death itself, largely, I suspect, because we don't want to think about it. We are learning never to underestimate the power of denial. Our American youth culture avoids the issue by experimenting endlessly with Dionysian vitalities of all sorts, from thundering rock music to the psychic transports of drugs, or the hope of some coming big score with a record or a book, or a dot com company. Dionysius is a god, and never dies. What this denial misses is that serious reflection on death, and the moral choices which that reflection inevitably confronts, are necessary for living the good life as a mature person. We are not children any more, so we do well to explore this irony of the human condition: that death holds a secret to life, even for those who do not believe in a life after death.

Our first section is on "Life, Death, and the Christian Hope," with essays by Peter Gomes, a preacher; Jürgen Moltmann, a theologian; and Rita Rainsford Rouner, a poet. We begin with the poet and her

1

reflections and poems on the death of her child. She starts by quoting, from the Book of Deuteronomy, God's promise to the righteous of long life and the presence of children who will inherit that blessing in their turn. But what if our children die before us? This is a disruption of the anticipated order of things. It is not supposed to happen, and parents suffer the guilt of survivors. Being a parent means that at least you don't let your children die. To explore this radical discontinuity in our lives, Rouner turns to the psychiatrist Robert Jay Lifton's interviews with Hiroshima and Holocaust survivors and his notion of "symbol formation"—the way we tell our own story to ourselves—as a means of survival. Having instinctively written a handful of poems after her son Timmy's death in a mountain climbing accident in Alaska in 1977, she finds that Lifton helps her understand something of what she was doing in this instinctive process.

Her subsequent poems chart a progression of different responses to a terrible event which never goes away. Her account is less a theory of those "stages of grief" with which we have recently become too familiar, than it is a surprised and grateful recognition of the way she has come since the day Timmy died. Beginning with the ecstatic celebration of "Into the Bright Immensities" and then plunging into the bleak depths of "Laments in October," she fights her way back to "Not a Sparrow Falls," an affirmation of God's presence for even the least of his creatures, and finally, "A Work of Spinning," in which she and Timmy continue from afar an intimate and unbreakable bond between two people whose love for each other was, from the beginning, made for eternity.

Our preacher, Peter Gomes, begins with a riff on the book's title, taken from the children's prayer "Now I lay me down to sleep" which was a daily part of his childhood bedside prayers. Gomes' concern as a pastor and preacher is how people live their lives before they die, so he proposes the question: "Knowing that we are to die, how shall we live?" Recognition of this question, he notes, is difficult to achieve in a culture which wants eulogies on these occasions so filled with "good stories of a good life, with so much good cheer and feeling, that it almost comes as a bit of rudeness to remember that all of that in this particular case has come to an end by reason not of retirement or sabbatical, but of death."

Traditional Christian liturgies, Gomes reminds us, took death seriously, not simply as the loss of life but as the occasion of judgment.

He traces the transition from the stern Calvinism of the seventeenth century when headstones were regularly marked by skulls and death's heads, or hourglasses and scythes, to the widespread mild Unitarianism of today, which replaces the terrifying day of doom with a day of warm and happy recollection, in which headstone figures of Grecian urns and stylized willow trees are the new symbols of memorial remembrance. What has been lost, Gomes believes, is a serious confrontation with the inescapable, unalterable fact of death itself, because "public and inconsolable grief is modernity's last and greatest taboo." He does not call for a return to Calvinism, or speculation about what Reinhold Niebuhr once called "the furniture of heaven or the temperature of hell." He looks, rather, to overcome our silence about death, and "recover the art of dying as part of the art of living."

Our theologian, Jürgen Moltmann, is also swimming against the contemporary stream in asking whether there is life after death and, if so, where the dead are. This is now a radical and awkward question because the once widespread Christian belief in life after death has itself suffered a slow death in our time, among church people and seminary professors. The respondent to the lecture from which this essay is taken was Gordon Kaufman, a professor of theology *emeritus* at Harvard Divinity School, who was vigorous in his rejection of the notion of life after death. If one were to poll theology professors from mainline Protestant seminaries on this question, I suspect that Kaufman's view would predominate. However, like Gomes, Moltmann gives weight to the tradition of the Church, and Paul's affirmation that faith and hope are crucial for the believer, even though love remains the greatest of all Christian virtues.

Moltmann emphasizes that the meaning of life after death is dependent on "a fulfilled life before death which we can affirm" and argues that the real issue is not between Platonic conceptions of an immortal soul and a mortal body, but between human understandings of love and death. "Can this loved, ensouled, and mortal life be immortal?" The issue for him is to see that immortality is to be ascribed not to a substance like the Platonic soul, but to a relationship of the whole person to the immortal God. Moltmann does not believe in Asian theories of reincarnation, nor does he subscribe to the Roman Catholic idea of purgatory, but he does believe in judgment. "God's judgment means the final putting to rights of the injustice which has been done and suffered, and the final raising up of those who are bowed down." Like

Calvin, Moltmann anticipates a great waking and watching of the soul after death in which it perceives its healing and its completion and experiences its rebirth for the life of a future world.

Our second group of essays concern views of life and death in various cultures, beginning with David Eckel's exploration of Buddhist views, under the wry title, "If I Should Die before I Am Awakened." Like Gomes, and so many others of his Protestant generation, Eckel was raised on this child's prayer, and he begins his essay with a lengthy exploration of its significance for the once ubiquitous *New England Primer* which taught generations of eighteenth-century American children the hopes and fears of the New England Protestant imagination, in the process of teaching them how to read. Eckel notes an analogy between the moral exhortations of the *Primer* and the rich tradition of storytelling in the Buddhist traditions of South and Southeast Asia, where the substance of that tradition was transmitted more through liturgical practice and storytelling than it was through direct instruction. The famous *Jataka Tales* deal with the previous lives and deaths of the Buddha, including animal tales such as the noble "king" of a deer herd who offers to sacrifice himself in order to save the herd.

No text is more relevant to his theme than the *Tibetan Book of the Dead*, a ritual guidebook recited to a person who has recently died to help that person's consciousness navigate the experiences of the afterlife. This three-stage process begins with a state of pure nondualistic awareness. In the second stage the person confronts the projection of their own fears and desires in a series of Buddha images. The third stage turns from the challenge of escaping the cycle of birth and death, to controlling the place where one will be reborn. Eckel emphasizes that the ritual intends not only to ease the dead person's passage into the next life, but to ease the thoughts and fears about death held by the living friends and relatives who perform the ritual. After summarizing the Pure Land tradition, and schools of Buddhist philosophy, Eckel reflects on the paradox involved in the Buddhist notion of reality as "emptiness." Here "awakening" to the unreality of immediate experience, including the experience of death, leads to a life free of fear and desire, lived in "the playful spirit of a child."

Brian Jorgensen's "A Rose for the Buddha" is in direct response to David Eckel's sympathetic presentation of Buddhism's view of life and death. Contemporary Western scholarship in religious studies tends to focus on appreciative understanding of those Eastern traditions which were severely criticized only a generation ago by Western

Christian missionaries and Western secular scholars alike. "Dialogue" among religious traditions, however, now requires a give and take, and value judgments. Jorgensen takes on the tricky task of appreciating both Buddhism and Christianity while edging toward an evaluation of these two different traditions. He does this through a comparison of the *Tibetan Book of the Dead* and Dante's *Inferno*, commenting that the Buddhist text is "moving, luminous, and post-humane." He explains: "I say 'post-humane' because the *Book of the Dead* denies the ultimate reality of what we ordinarily mean by human, yet could not properly be characterized as inhuman, or inhumane." He suggests that the Stoic coolness of the Buddhist view of life and death is less strange to us than the ancestral, antique religion of the *New England Primer*.

Dante's poem is a tale of "absent friends, and of coming to an understanding of what one once had, or once did, or once might have done." In this life after death we can expect to see these absent friends again, to understand what their lives were really all about, and to understand our own lives for the first time by seeing them in relation to the living transcendent mystery which is the reality of God. Tibetan Buddhism, on the other hand, celebrates the secret of all secrets, that there is no such thing as the self. "Emptiness" is the goal of life and death; detachment from the beloved is the key to the peace which passes all understanding. Jorgensen is careful not to make the contrast too stark. There is a "letting-go" in Dante which is not unlike Tibetan detachment. But are noble deeds, like the self-sacrifice of the deer king in the *Jataka Tales*, "illusions?—not deeds, nor great and humble presences, but pointers toward renunciations of self, useful little bridges toward the ultimate mercy of nonbeing? As such, then, not noble except as they contribute to the ultimate negation of the illusion of nobility?" Jorgensen finds it hard to think so, and he concludes, "What if the child's prayer 'If I should die before I wake/I pray the Lord my soul to take'—a prayer whose premise is, in many parts of the world, all too frequently true—might, in its petition as well as its premise, offer a glimpse, granted to us, not manufactured by us, of reality?"

This section on life and death in various religious cultures concludes with Wendy Doniger's question as to why people in stories choose mortality when they could have immortality. She divides them into two groups: those who choose mortal partners, and those who choose mortality for themselves. Of those who choose mortal partners there are four paradigms: (1) human men who prefer human women; (2) nonhuman women who prefer human men, (3) nonhuman men who prefer human women, and (4) human women who prefer human men. So, for example, Odysseus rejects Calypso and longs for home-coming and his wife, seemingly because Penelope lacks Calypso's end-less perfection. Later Doniger suggests that the case may be put the other way around: that humans, with their flaws, are more interesting than immortals and a life of bliss which cannot but become boring.

Doniger's wide-ranging exploration of myths in various cultures and time periods comes to rest in the popular culture of the contem-porary American cinema with her concluding question "Why did Dorothy want to leave Oz and return to Kansas?"—which is not unlike the question of Odysseus' longing for home. This question even both-ered the author of the Oz books who later had Dorothy return to Oz, along with Auntie Em and Uncle Henry, and become a Princess. In his account of the Oz mythology Salman Rushdie observes that "Oz finally *became* home; the imagined world became the actual world." Doniger doesn't have a philosophical answer to her own question, but she turns in conclusion to Yeats' "The Stolen Child," a poetic retelling of the folk-tale of the fairy changeling, and finds herself making the same kind of judgment that Jorgensen made. For Jorgensen the rejected bargain was that we gain the perfection of inner peace by emptying out all the sub-stance of human life. For Yeats' human child the bargain is to leave a "world full of troubles" that is "anxious in its sleep," a world "more full of weeping than he can understand" for a fairy world of the playful dance which appealed to David Eckel—a world where we "foot it all the night / Weaving olden dances, / Mingling hands and mingling glances" but where "He'll hear no more the lowing / of the calves on the warm hillside / Or the kettle on the hob / Sing peace into his breast. . . ." Doniger doesn't think the dance is enough, and she doesn't really like that kind of peace because it misses "the things that make human life precious."

In our final section on "The Philosophy of Life and the Problem of Immortality," the mood changes. No more loose association of myths and tentative conclusions. No more celebrations of empathy and pro-visional bows toward the other's point of view. No more affirmations of faith, endorsements of hope, poems of love. Now the issue is this: What does philosophy—the examination of belief in terms of logical analysis and empirical evidence—have to say about our theme?

We begin with John Lachs, whose empathy for human aspiration is matched only by his moral commitment to what we can actually know. Immortality is a vague human hope. Is it something that we have evidence for? Is it supported by a defensible logic? He begins by try-ing to understand this widespread human desire. It presupposes the standpoint of an isolated individual, since it is the individual in all his or her particularity which is to become immortal. There, Lachs tells us, is the rub. This popular notion of the self does not bear scrutiny. "Seeing individuals as separate from one another and confined within their bodies provides . . . a distorted picture of the facts." In truth "selves overlap and criss-cross in a multitude of ways, (so) it is not sur-prising that we take an intense interest in how we leave the world." "Death is horrible," he says, "not because it threatens non-existence, but because it cleaves the person and imposes an inevitable parting." The Buddhist joy in the peace of non-existence is clearly contrary to Lachs' philosophy of life. He is interested in what a self, with its indi-vidual identity intact, can reasonably hope for. Persuaded that we can only enjoy what is laborious and requires effort, he asks what notion of an afterlife would be viable.

It would need to be "a life that is problem-free and consists of an unbroken string of satisfactions. Such a heavenly existence would have to be social, but without the usual costs of communal life, that is, with-out friction, anxiety, destructive competition, conflicting interests and debilitating hatreds." He notes, immediately, that "we simply have no idea what such an existence would be like." Insofar as we can imagine a world of perfection it would be a painfully boring, deeply dissatisfy-ing world. His key point, however, is that "a heavenly afterlife sounds like a good idea, so long as we do not examine it enough to realize that there is not much of a concrete idea there at all." Worse than that, the desire for immortality is pernicious. It is a transcendent form of our current social and scientific drive to overcome all the difficulties stand-ing in the way of human fulfillment. The cost of such a "grand and fool-ish drive" is that we lose our souls. "We are finite creatures with lim-ited potential for satisfaction. . . . The infinite leaves us hungering for closure and sadly forgetful that everything is more precious when in short supply."

Aaron Garrett approaches the question of immortality by com-paring and contrasting the views of John Locke and Benedict Spinoza on the distinction between immortality and eternity. His title is taken from John Locke's epitaph, which Locke wrote himself. In it he makes a distinction between himself as an author who will be known posthu-mously through his writings, and what we might call the man himself, with his virtues and vices and his personal relation to his Savior. This distinction between the man and his work is analogous to the distinction between immortality and eternity. "Immortality is about transcending, moving past, moving beyond, being redeemed as against death." Eternity, on the other hand, is a much wider notion. Immortality is a concept enmeshed with death, and only those beings who could die could be immortal. Eternity has nothing to do with death. "If we are eternal, that part of us which is eternal will not die and never would die." The contrast between Locke and Spinoza—who were exact contemporaries and held many similar views—is highlighted by this distinction. Spinoza emphasizes eternity and tends to regard immortality as philosophically irrelevant. Locke, on the other hand, emphasizes immortality and has little to say about the kind of eternity so important to Spinoza.

This difference between them comes out most vividly in their moral theories. Both describe morals as "a naturally deducible system given what we know about human nature and human desires," but they are weighted very differently. "From the perspective of Spinoza's eternity, morals are hardly discernible, whereas for Locke they are a fundamental basis of the grant of immortality." For Spinoza, the consequence of one's eternity is that my immediate world of politics and morals is not part of my ultimate identity. As with the Buddhists, this did not mean eschewing morals or politics, but only recognizing that they were not ultimately serious. (Whether relief from engaged world-seriousness gave Spinoza a Buddha-like playfulness and lightness of heart, Garrett does not say.) For Locke, rational argument for immortality confronted the split between our weak and finite self-understanding and God's knowledge of us. Locke would have agreed with John Lachs that we can have no idea of what immortal life would be like. For Locke, however, the idea is central to his philosophy, crucial for morals, and in no way a pernicious loss of soul in a life which properly celebrates the finite.

David Roochnik begins his essay on "metaphorical immortality" with the bold assertion from Plato's *Symposium* that "mortal nature always seeks, as far as possible, to be immortal." This is Roochnik's good news. The bad news is that we don't ever actually get there. But perhaps it is not really bad news. Perhaps it points toward something crucial in human nature. Somewhere between Locke's rational belief in immortality and Lachs' persuasion that such belief can rob us of our souls, Roochnik proposes a view of metaphorical immortality which is not "merely" metaphorical because "talk about immortality captures something true about being human." His guide is Plato, and his starting point is the argument in the *Symposium* that genesis—primarily sexual reproduction—allows us to "participate" in immortality, although only in a metaphorical sense. Roochnik leaves aside the difficult question of what "participation" means in Plato, and turns rather to Socrates' arguments in the *Phaedo* for the literal immortality of the soul. In so doing Roochnik confronts the paradox that Plato seems to be arguing both sides of the issue of immortality.

What, then, can be said about the *Phaedo*? Roochnik presents a very careful analysis of the arguments and finds that none succeed. This raises the question of Plato's intent. Was he really intending to defend immortality literally and simply produced bad arguments; or was the failure of the arguments intended to demonstrate something else? Roochnik makes a good-humored confession: "Since I find it difficult to conceive of Plato doing anything badly, I much prefer the second option." His intent, however, is not an esoteric exercise in Plato scholarship, but to present a view of metaphorical immortality. His argument reminds one of Reinhold Niebuhr's paradoxical defense of biblical metaphors as symbols of a truth which they did not actually embody. The difference between Niebuhr and Roochnik, however, is that Niebuhr believed that biblical metaphors symbolized something transcendental which was literally true. Roochnik's view is also paradoxical: that to be human is to live precariously, "in-between" the negative flow of time and something that "is positive, and present, stable and always there even when we are not."

We conclude with David Schmidtz's reflections on "the meaning of life." He confesses at the outset that his background in analytical philosophy has not prepared him to answer questions about life's meaning, so he turns to autobiographical reflection as a way of coming close to the truth of his topic. In so doing he makes a rough distinction between Existentialist and Zen attitudes toward the question. Existentialism is desperate for meaning. If it cannot be found the Existentialist must choose between Stoicism and despair. The Zen attitude is that meaning is not something to be sought; it either comes to us or it doesn't, and we must learn acceptance, no matter what. Schmidtz is also impressed with Buddhist lightheartedness. He quotes Robert Nozick's suggestion that we regularly combine Existentialist and Zen attitudes. The question of life's meaning is so important to us, and leaves us feeling so vulnerable, that we camouflage our vulnerability with jokes about seeking the meaning or purpose of life. All those stories of seeking the sage in India only to get an inane answer are playful, but darkly so.

Schmidtz suggests modesty in our search for meaning. Meanings are always limited, they change, they need not be deep, and life is short. "Some things mean what they mean to me partly because of the price I paid for them. Other things mean what they do partly because they are gifts." One essential feature of meaningful lives, however, is that they have an impact. Further, meanings are symbolic, they track relationships, they are sometimes gifts and sometimes choices, and they track activity. "Life is a house" Schmidtz muses, and "meaning is what you do to make it a home." Schmidtz concludes with reflections on his own life. Twenty years ago he anticipated that in the year 2000 he would be a mailman somewhere in Canada, since that had been his work for four years, and he thought of it as an ideal job. Then he happened to read Hume's *Treatise*, and became a philosopher. For him, reflecting on his life is not a way of reaching a conclusion about its meaning, but just a way of getting a feel for it. There is no proposition one could write on a blackboard about the meaning of life. So he concludes with the comment that "one of the best things I ever did was coach little league flag football." He and his players had a mission. "There was no need to ask questions. There is no need now. The day was sufficient to itself, and so was the life."

There is a gap in this conversation between the philosophers on the one hand and the storytellers, theologians, and poets on the other. How might philosophical argument make a bridge to the transcendent? How might the insight of the poets and the faith of the theologians make a bridge to the rational world of the philosophers, in which we all live? We miss the presence of a thinker like Paul Tillich who had such a "bridge" metaphysics. This is not to say, however, that our essayists lack all common ground. All of them celebrate the human adventure and its values, even the Buddhists who must necessarily do so with metaphysical tongue in cheek. From Rita Rouner's love for her Timmy to David Schmidtz's little league coaching, there is a warm humanity here, along with a profound and logical love of life; and for that we have every reason to be grateful.

PART I

Life, Death, and the Christian Hope

A Short While towards the Sun: Poems and Reflections on Continuity and Loss, after the Death of a Child

RITA RAINSFORD ROUNER

I. INTRODUCTION: THE NEED FOR CONTINUITY

You shall keep his statutes and his commandments that it may go well with you, and with your children after you, and that you may prolong your days in the land which the Lord your God gives you forever. (Deut. 4:40)

You shall therefore lay up these words of mine in your heart and in your soul. . . . And you shall teach them to your children, talking of them when you are sitting in your house, and when you are walking by the way, and when you lie down and when you rise. And you shall write them upon the doorposts of your house and upon your gates, that your days and the days of your children may be multiplied in the land which the Lord swore to your fathers to give them, as long as the heavens are above the earth. (Deut. 11:18–21)

In the Old Testament book of Deuteronomy the commandments of God are delivered with an accompanying promise of a blessing which constitutes God's greatest gift to humanity: the gift of continuity. The highest demands for virtuous living come with an assurance of the highest fulfillment of that living, namely, long life and the presence of children who will inherit the promise in their turn. In making known to Israel the requirements for human living, God also promises that fulfillment will come with obedience, a fulfillment consistently associated with length of days and posterity.

An untimely death and the absence or loss of children are seen in the Old Testament as failure to reach fulfillment and therefore as a likely sign of judgment and of the withholding of God's blessing. Job struggles with incomprehension and despair when he notes that "the wicked live, reach old age, and grow mighty in power. Their children are established in their presence and their offspring before their eyes" (Job 21:7–8), while he, an upright God-fearing man, must endure the loss of his children, his health, and everything he values in life. With such destruction of all possible sources of continuity Job finds his life meaningless and abhorrent and is ready to give it up.

Life in the twentieth century has provided many people with comparable experiences of drastic loss and the destruction of continuity. The Nazi Holocaust, the atomic bombing of Hiroshima and Nagasaki, the killing fields of Cambodia, the genocide in the Balkans and in Africa have all confronted their victims with meaninglessness. The possibility of nuclear annihilation or biological extermination threatens the sense of meaning and hope for the future which is essential to keep present life from collapsing into the death-in-life of despair.

The psychiatrist Robert Jay Lifton has undertaken a study of the relationship between experiences of death and the struggle for continuity in human living. Profoundly influenced by his study of Hiroshima victims, he concludes that psychology has not given enough attention to "the psychological relationship between the awareness of death and the struggle for continuity."[1] He sees this relationship as the definitive paradigm for understanding the human situation and the structure and processes of the human psyche, especially given "the urgency of our present historical predicament."[2]

My concern here is to explore the themes of death and the struggle for continuity in relation to another experience which confronts people in a more private, individual way with a radical breaking of connection and with the threat of meaninglessness. This experience is the death of one's child. As with Job, when our children are taken from us all the purposes and meanings of our lives are called into question and put at risk.

It has been said that when our parents die we lose our past, but when our children die we lose our future. Certainly an enormous part of the life we had anticipated and hoped for is taken away from us when a child dies. And with it goes our sense of meaning, of what life was about for us. Our own life story seems suddenly aimless and without coherence now that our child's life story has ended. In his book *When Bad Things Happen to Good People*, Rabbi Harold Kushner writes that when he was told that his son was stricken with a rare and horrifying terminal illness, that discovery contradicted everything he believed about God, about the goals of human living, about "how the world was supposed to work."[3]

Our son Timothy was killed in August 1977 at the age of 19 in a mountain-climbing accident in Alaska. Since his death I have written a series of poems recording my own struggle to relate that death to my own continuing life.

Here I want to make a start at relating some general psychological principles to this profound personal experience which cannot be adequately described in psychological terms. Poetic and theological language can only point and suggest but never finally encompass the experience. I remind myself that all our encounters with the depths of existence, with death and with continuing life, are a mystery which cannot be fully communicated.

II. THE SYMBOLIZING PROCESS

A. *The Search for the Real*

Contemporary psychology and theology give increasing attention to the human need for symbol formation, the creation of forms and images by which we interpret experience. These forms and images become bearers of the continuity we seek, the means whereby we discover and recount the story in which we live.

This process of image making and symbol formation is an ongoing one which continues throughout the life cycle. Because human experience itself is a continuous, ever-changing process, the effort to give it form and meaning is also continuous. In telling our story we recount where we are now in relation to where we have been and where we expect to go. We create patterns, discard them, alter them, and recreate them as our life unfolds and presents us with new material to incorporate into our story. In the struggle to fashion adequate forms we search for continuity as a means to coherence. This search for adequate images to represent reality is a central human preoccupation.

Lifton describes the symbolizing process as "the mind's way of living in the world and the world's way of living in the mind."[4] He notes that our basic inclination as symbolizing human beings is toward increasing awareness. We have a hunger to take in deeper meanings and establish larger connections, to fashion our story in ever more inclusive ways. This human capacity for expanding awareness moves us toward a more ultimate kind of knowing.

The symbolizing process thus becomes a meeting place for psychology and theology, as both recognize the centrality of image making to the human enterprise. John McDargh, following Karl Rahner and Richard Niebuhr, defines the human person as a questioner, "one who interrogates being." He says, "There is a human grasping to know, i.e. to be in relationship to the real, which is as fundamental as the need for breath and bread." McDargh speaks of "the human yearning for communion with more and more reality" and suggests that this impulse toward more abundant living directs us beyond ourselves toward a transcendent dimension, a sense of connection with "that which is real, enduring and ultimately true."[5]

We know ourselves to have a story, a past, present, and future to give shape to and to hold in consciousness. Our images serve as maps which we use to determine our whereabouts and to find our way. Faith is the process of drawing up and then following these maps, of choosing the meanings we will use to understand and direct our lives. As our journeys continue, the maps may be found to be inadequate or misleading and so will need adjustment, or even to be erased and redesigned. But map making and map following is how we humans make our way in the world.

As the Book of Deuteronomy suggests, our children bring us not only the satisfactions and challenges of prolonged intimacy but also new windows on the world, new avenues to larger connection. These we may not always welcome, finding our established patterns threatened perhaps by the new realities of our children's stories, but our lives are enlarged and our horizons expanded by the presence of our children and by our connection to their ongoing journeys in the world.

In becoming parents we become participants in the ongoing story of humanity, links in the chain of generations joining an unremembered past to an unforeseeable future. Through our children and their children we know ourselves connected to dimensions of reality to which we have no direct access ourselves. Thus the experience of parenthood carries forward the human quest for more inclusive connections and for the sense of continuity which makes life seem worthwhile and blessed.

In rereading my poems about Timmy I note the varying images which represent his living presence in my world. "The wide-eyed heart running to meet the day," "the incandescent boy"—images of eager responsiveness to the surrounding world. "My lamb," " my tiger cub," "my leggy colt leaping through shimmering grass"—images of exuberant vitality and joy in life. The wild gander en route to far places which I will not visit. These and other images suggest for me awareness sharpened and life in the world enlarged by the close connection to the life of my child. It is ironic that often we only become fully aware of how richly we are blessed by the presence of our children in our lives when they are taken from us.

Here are two poems written in the fall after Timmy died.

Two Unlikely Deaths in a Usual Season

Our long-legged prancing son,
he of the tumbled curls
and the leaping laugh,
the wide-eyed heart running to meet the day,
has fallen off a mountain
and dropped unbelievably
out of the world.

And, as if this
were not hard enough to credit,
our old horse has died as well,
old trooper Dan,
who always jumped the pasture fence
when he suspected
others were leaving without him,
and had to be first out of the barn
and first on the trail
on a brisk autumn morning.

Now there are two new graves
on the New Hampshire hillside,
one by the leaning headstones
under monumental maples
and one in the open field
under milkweed and clover.

How can these two irrepressible beings,
the incandescent boy
and the exuberant old charger,
be now confined to earth and stillness?
Baffled, we too consider lying down,
submitting to snowfall
and the long cold sleep.

But no—
If we would meet them still
we must go romping afield.
I'm sure they have gone together down the lane ahead of us.
There where the leaves lie thick
they'll have just been by,
sniffing the sharp air,
harking to snapping twigs
and crows calling far in the treetops,
and ready for a rousing gallop
across the frosty meadow.
Timothy! Dan! We're coming.
We'll catch you up!

October 1977

Laments in October

I

All week long the sky has raged, distraught with grief.
The dark tempestuous weeping
tears from the trees
their tattered raiment
and tramples to sodden ruin
the summer's treasure.
O bitter anguish, helpless to recall
the passing season,
the fallen gold,
the young life lost
with the lost summer,
never to come again . . .
never again . .
never.

So have I too been given over
utterly to grief.
Beside the streaming pane
I have cried out for you
and, bleakly, have discovered
only your continuing absence. Hopeless,
I promise the unrelenting sky
that we shall be inconsolable forever and forever mourn . . .
forever . .
mourn forever.

II

Today the sky's grief is spent.
The strong sun climbs again,
And the dripping branches
wear meekly their nakedness.
Listless, I turn to common tasks
that wait in corners of my house.

Suddenly overhead it sounds:
the remote insistent clamor
that strikes the heart and drags it aloft
to cry with the geese the old urgent longing
now sharpened with loss.
The wavering banner presses toward the horizon
as necks thrust forward
and the light glints from laboring wings.
They carry their life southward,
exulting in the difficult, necessary voyage.
I tend mine here, bitter and bereft.

How should I rejoice again as they
now that your life has left us,
now that your journey has become
so hidden, so removed
that I cannot even glimpse your passage
nor hear you call down
like a wild gander
from some far bright archway of the morning
and know that you are glad
and on your way?

October 1977

B. Death as a Part of Reality

The reality with which we seek communion includes more than possibilities of fullness, of expanding connections and abundant life. It includes diminishment and separation. It includes mortality and death. To be in relation to the things of one's life involves necessarily the knowledge that one will die and that those to whom one is connected will die. Thus the relationship to life includes a relationship to death as a boundary, a limitation, as the mystery of finitude which forever accompanies the awareness of our humanity.

The story that we are engaged in living and trying to relate to in our meaning making is thus also a story of endings, of the loss and change of much that we are and value, and of the search for that which endures change and survives endings. As such, it is a story which evokes our fears and anxieties as well as our hopes and enthusiasms. It is a story we often prefer not to articulate. T. S. Eliot reminds us that, after all, "human kind cannot bear very much reality."[6]

The human condition of finitude and mortality drives us to search for connections which will survive the death we must anticipate, and transcend the limitations of our individual personal existence. It is the acknowledged awareness of death which sparks the search for continuity. In facing our mortality we yearn for an assurance of enduring transcendent meaning. Ernest Becker in *The Denial of Death* maintains that "in strictly psychological terms, then, the human person is a theological being."[7]

C. Unacceptable Death and the Threat to Continuity

The experience of parenthood, with its mystery of birth and its closeness to the growth of another person, provides us with a human experience which can convey transcendence. It is not without reason that Jesus, in speaking about God's unfailing commitment to human beings, spoke in terms of a parent relating to a beloved child. This image expresses most adequately the connection that nothing can sever. As parents we know that in the natural course of events we are destined to die while our children continue to live. There will be a separation to undergo. We may be saddened by this realization but it does not frighten or appall us nor put at risk the meaning of our parenthood.

If we are wise and loving parents we may expect that our children will be well able to live on in our absence, cherishing their memory of us and carrying on the continuing structure that is the family.

What we don't anticipate or allow for is the possibility that a child of ours will die while we still live. To experience that trauma gives rise to more than grief. It evokes denial and outrage and a desperate non-comprehension which is the opposite of awareness and the urge to respond. Rather than seeking to accommodate such an event as a measure of larger reality, we want to push it away and shut it out, refusing it any possible entrance into our story. "If that ever happened to me," sympathizing and frightened parents have said to me, "I couldn't live through it." Our sense of our own ongoing life is threatened by the very thought of such a violent disruption to our story, such an overturning of expected continuity by shocking discontinuity.

When, despite our refusal to admit the possibility, the unthinkable happens and a child dies, the effort to deny the reality of the event intensifies. We are stricken with panic. We struggle like a trapped animal to escape. We strike out in rage, wanting to place blame and seek revenge, to destroy something ourselves in protest and retaliation for the destruction that has come upon us. A few months after Timmy died I became preoccupied with the Greek figure of Demeter who, as a powerful goddess, was able to make her rage effective in the world and thus alter the situation and have her adored child returned to her. Demeter was the goddess of the earth and of the harvest. When her daughter Persephone was seized and carried off by Hades, the god of the Underworld, Demeter's intense grief brought winter upon the earth. Nothing could grow again until the gods of Olympus bargained with Hades for Persephone to be returned to her mother for part of every year. During this time Demeter rejoiced and the earth became fruitful again. I wrote this poem in January of the first winter after Timmy died.

A Myth Revisited

Now is the season when the goddess grieves.
The divine mother, robbed of her heart's treasure,
rages and mourns, inflicting her calamity
upon the earth.
The strong sun falters and withdraws.

The landscape cringes before armored cold.
Fields lie empty and barren trees
lift supplicating branches overhead.
There is no sustenance to be found,
no comfort under the wintry sky
while the sustaining fruitful mother
wanders comfortless about the land.
We shall not prosper while she tends her sorrow
remembering the dark thundering chariot,
the hawk-eyed lustful king,
the sudden yawning in the flowery meadow
and Persephone's arms flung back
in wild alarm.

O avenging mother, hear me!
Let mingle with your divine torment
this human pain.
Archaic female earth power,
I offer you my woman's woe,
my mother's need for aid.
I too have stood by, mute and impotent,
while my bright living joy was snatched away—
my lamb, my tiger cub,
my leggy colt leaping through shimmering grass,
my young eagle of the golden wings
and keen eyes seeing far and deep—
O stilled the restless legs, the eager wings!
O closed the shining penetrating eyes!

Like the treasured daughter spring-garlanded and merry,
all unmindful of danger,
careful and confident he climbed
throughout the long summer day,
until the god stood forth.
The mountain god, jealous, hostile
forbidding entrance to his solitary realm
where none had trod before
and smiting with fatal blow
the winsome young intruder.
So was he struck down,

fragile human body breaking
upon hard indifferent rock
within that alien kingdom of the mountain.

O Demeter, mother goddess, help me.
Not Persephone alone must be avenged.
Let the mountains forfeit now their beauty
in exchange for the stolen beauty of his life.
Enshroud forever the glittering summits
that summon men to glory and disaster.
Disguise the purity of that sharp thin air
that sets the blood pounding
before the heart is stopped.
Alter the majesty of towering rock and ice
to appear ugly and abhorrent,
repelling all questing spirits
rather than luring them
to risk everything in drawing closer.

So may all future sons, all ardent heroes
shun the earth's mountains
leaving them forsaken, forgotten, desolate,
deprived from now on of all human tribute:
heart's longing, spirit's fire,
mind's ambition, body's strength;
the joyous venture, the skilled endeavor,
the fearful courage, the willed endurance,
the continuing sustained passionate attention,
the living substance and the dead bones
of men.

                                          January 1978

When our rage is powerless to change anything we collapse into
frozen rigidity with the old responses to life deadened and inoperative.
This is the condition which philosophers and poets have described as
"death in life" or "life imitating death" and which Lifton calls "psychic
numbing."[8] The feeling response of grief to an encounter with death
as the inevitable and lamentable end of natural life is here replaced
by absence of feeling and inability to respond in any coherent vital way.
In this condition the attempt to exclude awareness of an outrageous

experience involves a repression of all awareness, a general abdication of feeling, and a separation from all forms of spontaneous vitality. The human person as responder becomes the human person as robot.

The language of common discourse reports that "the early days of anguish are a period no parent 'gets through'. It's just an existence of non-existence."[9] The conclusion that all meanings have been reversed and life made a mockery is unavoidable. This is the experience that I wrote of in this poem.

Survivor

I believe that all is well for you,
hurled headlong into eternity—
an arrow sped from the bowstring,
a bright drop flung from the cresting wave.
You climb on unimpeded now,
exploring new peaks and passes
in the great wilderness region
opening before you.
But I—
I hang from the cliff face where you fell,
dangling over the chasm,
staring with terror into the void
and clutching with bruised fingers
the unyielding rock.
I do not fall to sharp releasing death
nor do I hope for rescue,
to be removed to some safe grassy slope
and find the trail again.

No, this is my station
now that you are gone:
this harsh precarious place of grief,
this locus of suspended danger,
swaying in the empty air
against the sheer wall
that looms against the light
and plunges to unfathomed dark.
Here no movement is safe,
no action possible.
Here I hover,

weak with vertigo,
frozen with fear,
between the abyss and the unrecoverable surface.
From here it seems that you are the one
who lives
and I, immobilized,
the one who is caught in death.

October 1977

III. THE WORK OF SURVIVAL

When our encounter with the world is overwhelmingly traumatic
and destructive of the forms we have used hitherto to order our experience, we become blocked and lose our ability to fashion the new
forms required to incorporate the new experience. Thus, psychic
numbing leaves us without images and patterns of meaning. In reading accounts of the reactions of parents to the death of their children,
I am struck with the extent to which these accounts report lack of feeling and gaps in awareness. Repeatedly the stories tell of inability to
remember the funeral and the events of the following days, even
weeks; inability to grasp the fact that the child is not there any more;
inability to make decisions or plan ahead; inability to feel anything
other than a vague anxiety and numbness.

In the winter after Timmy died I wrote this poem.

Reproach from the Sinuses

Of course life must go on.
Agreeing, I hurried about
Steering the car along the usual routes,
Waving at neighbors' children,
Carrying groceries into the kitchen—
I forgot the toothpaste again
Though I did remember
to buy one less chop.
So I bustled around the edges
of my life,
while at the hidden center
grief sat still,
waiting and unattended.

O implacable guest,
you were not slow to take offense.
While I persisted, heedless of your presence,
You stored your undelivered burden
in buried cisterns that swelled in secret.
The tears filled up inside my head,
the unshed tears,
pressing against the eyes
and under the cheekbones
until,
diagnosed acutely infected,
I must give up
these distracted comings and goings
and stay at home,
swallowing pills
and holding hot cloths to a throbbing face
til the living vessels crack
and the captured waters
seep to the surface.

Better to have come straight in
from the new grave
and closed the door
and drawn the shades
and settled down to weeping
as long as tears remain,
which may be
                for all
                    the rest
                        of my
                            days.
                    February 1978

   It is at this point that the work of survival is engaged. The struggle toward inner form must be taken up again if life is to continue with
vitality. The survivor must now know herself to be precisely that: one
who has encountered death and who survives. Her story, her images of
self and world must be enlarged to include this new overwhelming
knowledge.

At first such a re-forming of one's images and meanings seems impossible. As we are able to grasp the nature of the task our resistance to it is renewed. The impulse is to insist on denial, to prefer death-in-life to the ongoing life which can continue only by giving form and thereby acknowledgement to the unacceptable death. But as the survivor realizes that she is in fact a survivor and endures the shock of that realization, the creation of new images becomes possible, images which now include this radical knowledge. The self, painfully opened to knowing itself to be a survivor of the encounter with death, takes up again the process of formulation. Thus, in the renewed struggle for symbols and images adequate to the new situation, psychic life moves forward again and the life story continues to be fashioned. It is a story which now includes the account of death and the threat of discontinuity. It has become a story of the search for viable forms of continuity which can survive that threat. Death now becomes a source of creativity and enlarged vision rather than a source of disintegration and impairment of the life process. Psychic numbing is gradually replaced by a renewed and more powerful imagination.

A transformed relationship to death as teacher and enabler of larger life does not occur readily or completely. The renewed struggle for viable forms must begin with images of destruction, with an account of the breaking of old connections and the loss of continuity, with the painful details of the experience which psychology labels desymbolization, the loss of former meaning and coherence. The survivor is inevitably and rightly suspicious of false assurances. To be urged to focus on positive images which minimize or distract from the shattering impact of death is to have one's shaky efforts at resymbolization undermined. It is disturbing rather than comforting to be prompted to be thankful for one's remaining children as one struggles to integrate into one's life the continuing absence of the one who has died. During the Advent season following Timmy's death I wrote this poem:

Invocation in Advent

How shall we pass this way this year?
How consider the birth of a divine child
when our knowledge stretches and cracks
to include the death of the bright earthly boy?
How strain to catch angelic harmonies

when our ears ring with the harsh sound of grief?
Why visit the glowing manger
when in our hearts so great a light is quenched?
Where can room be found for a tiny joy
amidst such enormous pain?

This is the time of waiting in the night.
The cold tightens and the dark advances.
Skilled in survival but stricken now, we learn
that this is no seasonal darkness,
no passing nadir of the turning year,
but final irretrievable loss,
devastation not to be rebuilt.

The old machinery founders on this death.
The natural cycle of revived expectation
following replayed defeat,
wheat springing green in the wintry furrows,
the tested equipment making it possible
to proceed through periods of privation
and the recurring desert spaces:
all this is shattered and lies about us
littering the ground with shapeless fragments.
Death is a young broken body
and an old broken pattern of living,
both ruined beyond repair.

What new infant hope can come to birth
within this desolation?
If there is some crack, some hidden corner,
some overlooked insignificant spot
where the unlikely miracle
can find room to happen,
let it take place.
We withhold for a breath our bleak lamenting
and wait, attentive and disbelieving,
to be surprised.

                              December 1977

    After Timmy died I found that writing poetry was a way of mov-
ing on and taking my experience with me. Searching for images to rep-

resent the many-sided reality of his death, I was able to make that reality more completely part of my life and to have a fuller relationship to it than I could have had otherwise. It was as important to record the experience of disruption and discontinuity as it was to search for new possibilities for continuity. The "crystal pitcher in shattered pieces," the foundering of the "old tried machinery, now littering the ground with shapeless fragments," the infected sinuses sabotaging the attempt to go on as though things were the same, the family ritual of the weekend evening meal, carefully enacted and bringing no healing after all: these images point to the broken connection, the radically disintegrating effect of death. According to Lifton, it is "this capacity for intimacy with (and knowledge of) death in the cause of renewed life which is the survivor's special quality of imagination, his special wisdom."[10]

I wrote this poem the second winter after Timmy died.

Return to the Farm in Winter

Around the old house darkness falls.
Snow heaped against windows
and stretching across empty fields.
Inside the fire crackles;
pots bubble on the stove
chuckling their tales of spicy contentment
and announcing that the ancient magic holds:
Around steaming platters and dark poured wine
the family will be reconstituted—
one fabric despite the jagged hole
torn in the cloth,
circle completed in the candlelight
however dim the shadowed segment.
Here in this place called home
our lost one lingers.
Here we have brought our mute unending woe,
intent to recover the remembered solace
in the repeated rite,
the familiar sacrament that has kept us whole
through many other winters.

The meal is ready.
We are summoned and come, hungering, hopeful.

The food is savory, soothing our anxious flesh
and publishing its satisfaction in our midst.
Talk and laughter sound in the listening air
reporting that life continues
eventful and engaging as before.
Wary of forgery, we are not taken in
by mind's distraction or stomach's ease.
Bleakly we note that emptiness remains,
silence is unrelenting and
the hope of healing drains away.

The meal is finished.
We do not move.
On the disheveled table candles dwindle,
ebbing flames reflected in eyes that utter
wordlessly the truth between us:
the old ritual no longer serves.
We are not nourished, not restored
by the enacted remedy.
Haunted by his absence now,
we know ourselves diminished, damaged, maimed,
afraid to look directly at the scars.
Instead we glance persistently backward
fondling lost occasions,
caressing the sweet shape
of a remembered life.
Ahead is an empty space.
We cannot imagine its landmarks
and shrink from stepping forward
on newly crippled limbs
into the void.
After a while we draw apart and sleep.

Later above the cold dark hills
dawn flames;
with streamers brightening the waking sky
another day begins.

                                        February 1979

V. CONCLUSION: THE POSSIBILITY OF TRANSFORMATION

In the poem written in Advent, I conclude with the moment of waiting for the uncreated new form which can include the life-threatening death and transform it into a source for continuity. The imagery of Advent helps to identify such a moment: the time of darkness, of waiting for a new birth, of not knowing exactly who to expect or where to watch for the arrival. It is the biblical witness that it was indeed a "hidden corner, [an] overlooked insignificant spot where the unlikely miracle [did] find room to happen." The Gospel story helps us, amid present devastation, to "withhold for a breath our bleak lamenting and wait, attentive and disbelieving, to be surprised."

As I lived on in the reality of that broken connection, and in the waiting which the Advent poem expresses, I became aware of images other than those of loss and separation making their presence felt in my imagination. From the start there were also images of continuity and enduring connection which were part of the encounter with Timmy's death. The earliest poem recounts the accident and is a poem which seemed to arrive complete and of itself like a direct word from Tim about his experience of falling to his death on the mountain.

Into the Bright Immensities

The fall was fatal.
The towering summit soared
into the glowing sky
and the lower face dropped away
in shadowed ridges.
You slid swiftly down the snowy slope
and tumbled off into the vibrant air,
crashing like a cataract
upon the ledge below.
Leaving your ruined young body,
a crystal pitcher in shattered pieces,
you pranced off
into the enormous spaces
waiting to receive you.

> The evening brimmed the world with radiance.
> On the dark ledge your forsaken brother,
> raging with grief,
> drenched your dead face
> with tears and kisses;
> while you, altered but whole,
> romped up the sunlit peak
> to stride the spired skyline
> and dance upon the pinnacles,
> laughing and throwing back kisses
> and shouting down the splendors of the view.
>
>   September 1977

I was enormously grateful for the gift of this imagined picture of him, so recognizable in his vitality and responsiveness and his readiness to share.

Christian faith offers many images of God's unfailing care and protection which become enlivened when we are threatened with death. The image of the God who cares for the sparrow provided me with a vivid picture of Timmy being ministered to in the moment of falling to his death by One who "holds in dear safekeeping each one who falls."

Not a Sparrow Falls

"They were under the sway of noble and profound thoughts . . . and feeling of peace and reconciliation. Everything was transfigured as though by a heavenly light and everything was beautiful, without grief, without anxiety and without pain." (Albert von St. Gallen Heim, *Remarks on Fatal Falls*)

"Are not two sparrows sold for a farthing? and one of them shall not fall to the ground without your Father. . . . Fear not, therefore; you are of more value than many sparrows." (Matt. 10:29–31)

> Under the frozen shrubbery
> by the subway entrance
> at the edge of the park
> a handful of bedraggled feathers,
> a limp curled claw,

and a small bright eye closing
to the impartial light.
A few ounces of intense life
flutters and subsides
while the massive city
pursues its turbulent career.
No fellow creature notes this tiny death.
It is of no consequence,
a non-event.
But we are told
that the deep burning gaze of angels,
eyes shining amid throbbing wings,
splendor streaming from the divine center—
all the ardent unwavering attention
of the Holy One
is focused upon this spent morsel,
this precious fallen scrap
of a beloved creation.

So be it!
Now I know that when you fell
on that far mountainside
beneath impassive stony peaks
with no one watching,
no other soul aware
in that dread instant
that your life was hurtling downward
to destruction,
you did not fall alone.
The rush of empty air around you
surged with wings,
wheeling, shimmering,
bending to touch your flying hair.
From the blind rock arose a host
whose eyes poured forth a blaze of love
to fold your plunging limbs in light.

So were you arrayed for death
in the summoned glory of heaven
and in that lone unwitnessed passage

were surely kept and cradled
in infinite promised mercy,
father-steadfast, mother-tender;
were surely companioned
by the watcher who misses nothing,
who holds in dear safekeeping
each one who falls.

February 1978

Since so much of parenting involves our human effort to keep safe the young life entrusted to us, much of the anguish of the bereaved parent is the sense of having ultimately failed in that responsibility. The image of a God who is present in danger when we are far away, and able to help when we are helpless, gives us an assurance of continuity with our own parental work so that the meaning of our care for this child is not destroyed because we were unable to protect him from death.

When a child dies, the struggle for continuity, as we have seen, is radically threatened. Likewise the search for some form of symbolic immortality becomes intensified in relation to the child who is gone. As time passes we find that the relationship so central to our life continues even though the living child is no longer present. William James observed that "there persists in the human consciousness a sense of reality, a feeling of objective presence, a perception of what we might call 'something there.'"[11] It is this sense of reality which provides the experiential ground for our beliefs about God and about the reality of the transcendent. The sense of a continuing relationship to someone who has died is an instance of such an experience of presence. Christianity interprets such an experience as a witness to God's power to overcome death and preserve for eternity the bonds of love.

In forming images of an ongoing relationship with a beloved child now dead we carry on a conscious relationship with that child. He remains present in our lives as a living being, so that his death alters but does not destroy the reality of that relationship. Four years after Timmy's death I wrote of the constant changing connection that represents our relationship to one another. Following the theme of a connecting cord, images of the linking of our lives unfolded in the poem. First the umbilical cord joining the unborn infant to the expectant mother. Then the looser, longer rope, woven from the years of lived intimacy. Then the rending separation, the failure of the living link, when he was suddenly torn away. After that, across the distance dividing the living from the dead, the sense of communication across the separating gulf, ensuring our continuing connection. I wrote this poem in Maine in the summer of 1981.

A Work of Spinning
for T.N.R.

Under the soft sky of another summer
on this northern coast
the thread was begun,
while sea fog drifted through the spruce tops
and wild roses smoldered on the point.
Secret spinning
in the dark hollow
between bones shaped
to cradle life,
like the inner curve of a shell.

Nine times the moon increased and withered,
the cold came on . . withdrew,
while the thread swelled
to a blue-veined cord
throbbing between worlds,
connecting what was coming
to what had gone before,
a warm lush cable
humming with messages between us.

I remember this season and this place.
I remember the wonder of my body
enfolding your body,
my new astounding skill
to spin your unknown substance
from my own,
to fashion without thought or effort
the connecting cord.

At the appointed moment
the blue rope was discarded.
Together then we spun another
just as strong
but looser, longer,
devised with deft movements of
holding and letting go,
weaving the countless ways we found
of touching:
first your small fingers tucked in mine,
later your strong hands
taking up tools to clear a trail
to the hilltop behind the house,
leading me
to view the mountain.

For nineteen summers we spun
until, at another moment
perhaps likewise appointed,
on a mountain far from me
another blue rope coiled unavailing
on your brother's shoulder,
you were ripped from all moorings
and flung out
into vast spaces
beyond reach of any line.

Now I begin again
under a brightening sky
where the cold sea stirs
and presses against granite,
a new spinning,
solitary, austere,
no more the spontaneous work of flesh
but slow deliberation of the spirit.
I gather up untried strands
to weave once more an unknown substance
out of new touchings,
trails to other viewpoints.
I remember

how we spun together
and wonder if you too
are twisting to a shining length
some starry fabric you have now discovered
to toss to me
as I work on alone.
                    Hardscrabble Hill, Maine   July 1981

Writing this poem was a very important undertaking for me. The images simmered in my mind for over a year before I tried to give them precise form. Shaping that poem enabled me to become more fully connected to many things in my life and world, just as Timmy's living presence had been a source of vitality and fullness for me. The sense of our abiding connection survives loss of that living presence and gives me new heart for my own continuing life, for the weaving of new substances and the following of "trails to other viewpoints."

The lines from Stephen Spender with which I have titled this essay articulate the same experience of a relationship which survives the separation of death. Spender's poem, "I Think Continually of Those Who Were Truly Great," speaks of how those vital, inspiring people who have been taken from us continue to make available more fullness and vitality for those who remain after them. The very vividness of their presence in our lives endures in the images associated with them which live on in our souls and continue to inspire, comfort, and guide. In a compelling poetic image Spender conveys the reality of their continuing connection to us. They have left us after a brief time in our midst, but the very air from which we continue to take breath and life carries their impact and continues to convey to us their presence and their power. Spender's poem concludes with these lines:

Near the snow, near the sun, in the highest fields,
See how these names are fêted by the waving grass
And by the streamers of white cloud
And whispers of wind in the listening sky.
The names of those who in their lives fought for life,
Who wore at their hearts the fire's centre.
Born of the sun they travelled a short while toward the sun,
And left the vivid air signed with their honour.[12]

NOTES

1. Robert Jay Lifton, *The Broken Connection* (New York: Basic Books, 1979), p. 4.

2. Robert Jay Lifton, *The Life of the Self* (New York: Simon and Schuster, 1976), p. 27.

3. Harold S. Kushner, *When Bad Things Happen to Good People* (New York: Schocken Books, 1981), p. 3.

4. Lifton, *Life of the Self*, p. 65.

5. John McDargh, *Psychodynamic Object Relations Theory and the Study of Religion* (New York: University Press of America, 1983), p. 49.

6. T. S. Eliot, "East Coker."

7. Ernest Becker, *The Denial of Death* (New York: Free Press; London: Collier Macmillan, 1975), p. 38.

8. Lifton, *Broken Connection*, p. 47.

9. Katherine Fair Donnelly, *Recovering from the Loss of a Child* (New York: Macmillan, 1982), p. 22.

10. Lifton, *Life of the Self*, p. 130.

11. Quoted in McDargh, *Psychodynamic Object Relations Theory*, p. 118.

12. Stephen Spender, "I Think Continually of Those Who Were Truly Great," in *Collected Poems, 1928–1953* (New York: Random House, 1955), p. 32.

Death and the Believer:
The End Is Where We Start From
PETER JOHN GOMES

SLEEP AND DEATH

One of the long-standing comparative cliches of our time has been
that the Victorians were obsessed with death and inhibited by sex,
and that we are obsessed with sex and intimidated by death. As with
most cliches, there is enough truth here to allow us a useful beginning
to a conversation whose title, "If I Should Die . . ." is drawn from perhaps the most prominent example of Victorian popular piety, the children's bedside prayer "Now I lay me down to sleep. . . ." I was brought
up on this prayer, whose rather grim theology cast no shadow upon my
uncomprehending slumbers:

> Now I lay me down to sleep,
> I pray the Lord my soul to keep:
> If I should die before I wake,
> I pray the Lord my soul to take.

Another, older version of the same prayer reads:

> Now I lay me down to sleep,
> I pray the Lord my soul to keep:
> Four corners to my bed,
> Four angels there aspread;
> Two to foot and two to head,
> And four to carry me when I'm dead.
> If any danger come to me,
> Sweet Jesus Christ deliver me;
> And if I die before I wake,
> I pray the Lord my soul to take.

We can see how the older version made much more explicit the consciousness of death, complete with ministering angels and transport to heaven; and musicians will recall the adaptation of this version in "The Children's Prayer" in Englebert Humperdink's nineteenth-century opera *Hansel and Gretel*. The shorter version is perhaps the more familiar one. At its close there usually followed a litany of particular blessings upon family and friends, and the anticipated crisis of the next prepubescent day. Inherent in both versions of this bedside prayer, however, are a number of theological assumptions whose psychological implications might not now pass muster with post-Spockian theories of child-rearing. First among them is the notion that the soul is at risk during slumber. Waking, we are aware of the dangers and risks to our soul, after which Satan is always on the prowl. Any Christian child would have been made familiar with the Pauline images of the activist Satan seeking whom he may devour, and to be awake is to be aware of this constant risk, and therefore to be prepared to defend against it. When we sleep, that is, when we come to rest, we let down our natural defenses. This does not mean that Satan ceases to be engaged, for in fact it means that we are at greater risk, and hence the need to commend the duty of safeguarding the soul to the Lord.

It is not the notion of Satan, however, or even of the contest for the soul of the child, that is so startling here. What gets our attention is the phrase "If I should die before I wake." The possibility of death is introduced at our most vulnerable moment, for sleep is the anticipation of death. Few of us contemplate the very real possibility that when we go to sleep we may not wake up, for we have appointments to keep, and alarms to help us keep them. We assume the morrow, for we must. Even though there are seasons of vulnerability when we are ill, in hospital, aged, alone, and afraid, still we ordinarily suspend the reality of the possibility of death. What is alarming and arresting about this bedtime prayer is that it does not do so.

It further assumes that the most precious thing we have is not our life, but our soul. It is our soul that we pray the Lord to keep should we lose our life in the night. The prayer does not ask to be preserved from death. It does not ask for safe passage from one day to the next. It acknowledges the reality of death, the possibility that death may come to us unprepared, and it therefore seeks to safeguard that which is even more precious than life: the soul. All of that is a great deal to pack into a little bit of bedside doggerel, but there it is.

It is not my purpose to deconstruct this prayer after the fashion of much of postmodernist criticism, so that in "understanding" it we destroy it for all useful purposes. My subject is not the soul, nor is it immortality, nor is it even warfare with Satan. As a Christian pastor and preacher I am interested in how death affects the way believers live before they die, for life after death is one of the big issues of Christian theology and there is much written on this topic. For nearly a century Harvard has offered the Ingersoll Lectures on Immortality, by which we have not been much edified on the subject of life after death and the immortality of the soul: anyone can discourse on the subject of life after death, but all of us have to live life *before* death, and for Christian believers that is the real challenge and the real issue. Knowing that we are to die, how shall we live?

DEATH AND DENIAL

For nearly thirty years I have had the duty of conducting memorial services for my colleagues in The Memorial Church at Harvard University. They are stately affairs, constituting as they do the last tribute of colleagues and friends to a departed member of an official family. I early on learned not to confuse these occasions with funerals, and I was often reminded that the emphasis here should be on life and not on death. Funerals had become private, even furtive things, done as quickly as decency allowed, while a memorial service was both a right and a rite, a summing-up of this particular life's accomplishments, usually by colleagues and, on occasion, by family as well. I remember one of the most senior members of the University coming to me after one service and saying in the conditional tense, "Should I die . . ." and then indicating his wishes for me to carry out in some indeterminate future.

Death in the university is something of an unwelcome intrusion in a community that prides itself on youth and continuity; it is the great discontinuity, the unwelcome guest, and it is understandable that we should seek to minimize its presence among us. The eulogies on such occasions are usually so filled with good stories of a good life, with so much good cheer and feeling, that it almost comes as a bit of rudeness to remember that all of that in this particular case has come to an end by reason not of retirement or sabbatical, but of death.

The denial of death is even more true among the young. I have officiated at more than my share of services wherein the lives of students taken tragically from them are celebrated in our church, and those occasions are seasoned in almost equal parts by grief, anger, and incredulity. Death here is not impartial: it is unfair.

IN THE MIDST OF LIFE

In the Burial Office of the Book of Common Prayer, when the people come to the grave, the minister customarily reads a set of sentences which includes a paragraph from the old Sarum Rite: "In the midst of life we are in death; of whom may we seek for succor but of thee, O Lord, who for our sins art justly displeased?" Christian burial has at its heart two facts disagreeable to the modern sensibility, those of sin and of death. The original notion of comfort—that is, the offering of strength or fortitude as opposed to mere sympathy or consolation—had to do with the promise of forgiveness of sins as a prerequisite to the avoidance of damnation or the eternal death. The Prayer Book Office, for example, prays for the deliverance from "the bitter pains of eternal death." That death is not just the end of mortal life, but the eternal separation from God after that death. The cause of the first death may well be those things to which the flesh is heir: disease, age, accident; but the second, the eternal death, has as its cause sin, which can be remitted only by the merciful action of God. Hence the traditional emphasis at Christian burial was not on the consolation of the living but on intercession for the soul of the departed. Contrary to the now fashionable cliche that "funerals are for the living," Christian burial was in substance and fact expressly for the dead, and for the dead's destiny after death.

Perhaps the most vivid liturgical example of this emphasis upon death as the occasion for the judgement of sins is the *Dies Irae* or "Day of Wrath" of the old Roman Requiem Mass. It is a description of the judgement together with a prayer to Jesus for mercy, drawn in part from the Old Testament book of Zephaniah (1:14–16), and adapted in the eighteenth century for liturgical use by Thomas of Celano. Arranged in eighteen verses, each increasingly vivid in its depiction of the final judgement, the final verse offers the note of intercession around which the funeral office is constructed:

Ah! that day of tears and mourning!
From the dust of earth returning,
Man for judgement must prepare him;
Spare, O God, in mercy spare him!
Lord, all pitying, Jesus blest,
Grant them thine eternal rest.

Those old enough to remember the pre-Vatican II Roman Requiems will recall the constructed terror of the rite. The liturgical color was black, the coffin was surrounded by six black candles, the music was solemn, and the mood intimidating. Something of that mood is yet available to those who are familiar with the great musical settings of the Requiem by Mozart, Verdi, Beethoven, and Berlioz. Even the transcending Gallic beauty of the setting of Faure has at its heart the *Dies Irae*.

Death was meant to be taken seriously, not simply as the loss of life but as the occasion for judgement. Our sympathy was meant not so much for the living as for the dead, for whom now the day of judgement could not much longer be postponed. Thus, when the priest intoned "In the midst of life we are in death . . ." he meant to communicate the illusory nature of life itself, the inevitability of death, and the fear not so much of death, but of what the father confessors called "death unprepared," that is, dying in such a state as to insure a less than favorable judgement on the other side. It was to address the fear of "death unprepared" that the Roman sacrament of Extreme Unction, the so-called "last rite," was introduced. It was the object of the faithful to die in as close to a state of grace as possible, so as to provoke the mercy of God in judgement.

Anyone who has ever read, or watched the film version of, Evelyn Waugh's very Catholic novel *Brideshead Revisited*, will recall the length and intensity of the deathbed scene of Lord Marchmain. Here was a British aristocrat who had made a nominal conversion from Anglicanism to Catholicism in order to marry a devout Roman Catholic woman. He had then deserted her and her religion, after World War I, to live in an adulterous relationship in Venice with a beautiful Italian mistress. After the death of his wife on the eve of World War II, he returns to his ancestral home to die. The energy of the deathbed scene is to persuade the nearly comatose Marchmain to accept the last rites of the Roman Church. He refuses to do so, but at the end, when the simple parish priest pleads with him to make a sign of his repentance, his sorrow for offending God by his sins, he makes a feeble but recognizable sign of the cross, and then expires, commended by the priest to the mercies of God. It is this death, with its powerfully symbolic reconciliation of the worst of sinners with a merciful God, that affects the course of the lives of all of the principals in the story. It is not so much the apparent triumph of a powerful superstition over a rational and secular world, as the observing Charles Ryder might suggest. Even he in his doubt comes to the view that, however late in time, for this family in which he has become enmeshed the consciousness of death has become the force by which their lives have been and will be governed; and that transaction between life and death is the province of faith as expressed in the rites and sacraments of the church. He leaves the scene, if not believing, at the least deeply wondering—which is one of Waugh's least subtle ambitions.

When I was a child, fifty-five years ago, it was still a common experience in the small New England town of my youth to see mourning wreaths on the front doors of houses in which a death had recently occurred. The presence of the wreath meant that the body of the deceased was still within the house, and that the family was prepared to receive visitors. This was an age in which home funerals were still common. The obituary notice often carried the phrase that the funeral would be held "from the late residence of the deceased." Among the older generation of that era black mourning bands for the men and mourning dress for the women were still customary, and printers and stationers kept a supply of black-bordered stationery with which the mourning family would conduct its social correspondence for at least a year and, for certain widows, forever. To this day at Harvard black-bordered cards are sent out by the President's office to announce the deaths of members of the University.

Today it is the accepted fashion to minimize the public notice of death, and almost rude to imply mourning by any outward sign, which suggests that to acknowledge the dead in this way would spook the living. Most people who in earlier days would have descended immediately into deep and public mourning are today encouraged to "get over it and get on with it"; and, alas, it is quite possible to sit next to a co-worker and have no knowledge of the fact that a death has occurred in his or her immediate family. The formal expression of written condolences is itself a dying art, and the etiquette of death has become increasingly sanitized and efficient.

SKULLS, CHERUBS, AND WILLOWS

Many years ago, as a young librarian of The Pilgrim Society in Plymouth, Massachusetts, I was invited to assist in an anthropological study of the headstones in Burial Hill, the graveyard which served Plymouth from the seventeenth through the late nineteenth century. At least two Pilgrim Fathers are buried there, Governor Bradford and John Howland, and a great host of their descendents. The anthropologists were interested in the iconography of the stones during the period from 1660 to 1820, noticing three prevailing patterns which corresponded roughly to the three centuries in question. The seventeenth-century stones were often marked with grim skulls and death's heads, with hourglasses and scythes, symbols of fleeting and arbitrary time, often found as related motifs. By the middle of the eighteenth century the death's heads had become benign, even smiling, cherub heads; and angels with wings were a quite common design. By the first quarter of the nineteenth century all such figural representations had disappeared in favor of memorial Grecian urns and stylized willow trees, well-known symbols of memorial and remembrance. I was asked if I could provide any theological interpretation of these transitions, and this was not hard to do as the iconography followed fairly closely the theological transitions in the parish church, from a strict Calvinism through a mild Arminianism to a liberal Unitarianism. Art followed conviction, and these convictions moved from a concern with the life to come both positive and negative to the memory of the life now departed. The day of doom has been replaced—if not by the day of resurrection, at the very least by the day of recollection. A much more comprehensive study in which this phenomenon is included is to be found in Alan Ludwig's classic work on American funerary art, *Graven Images*.

Liturgically, something of the same thing has occurred. The reform of the funeral liturgy in the Roman Catholic Church after Vatican II is a vivid example of the wholesale transformation of the relation of the dead to the living. The color, for example, is no longer black, but white. The liturgical emphasis is no longer upon the "Day of Wrath," the impending judgement upon the dead with its inevitable anticipation of the same for the living, but upon the resurrection and the promise of new and everlasting life. Even the Roman liturgy now allows for that most prominent of Protestant funeral "rights," the eulogy, or memorial address. The funeral homily is meant to instruct the faithful and the not-so-faithful in the Church's teaching about sin, death, and judgement, and to be an occasion for what the Anglican prayer book calls the "amendment of life," while the eulogy places the emphasis upon the life of the departed, and the precious element of memory. Instead of commending the dead to judgement and the grave, the eulogy tries to recapture the life of the departed, often with intimate and funny anecdotes, in one last effort to defeat the obvious accomplishment of death. In many contemporary funerals, even in Roman Catholic rites, it is possible to forget the facts of death in an atmosphere of jolly recollection and friendly fellowship. Grief, if it is permitted at all, is directed to the untimely loss of the deceased; it is hardly permissible to express grief at what may happen to the deceased after death, for the secular sensibility would regard such an expression as "too morbid," which is a strange indictment of a funeral. Long gone from our contemporary consciousness is John Henry Newman's rather acute summary of the human condition: "Life is short. Death is certain. And the world to come is everlasting."[1]

THREE FUNERALS

The utter contradiction of this view can be seen in perhaps the most widely experienced funeral in human history, that of the late Diana, Princess of Wales. Millions watched as her service was conducted from Westminster Abbey: the public grief which surrounded it was nearly universal, and to this day defies adequate analysis except as an example of cathartic, therapeutic, or "good grief," *en masse*. The service, however, was a splendid example of an evolving new etiquette of death. First, it was a remarkable eclectic occasion: neither fully state nor fully private. Her precarious public position as an ostracized member of the Royal Family forbade the state occasion to which many felt she was entitled; and her popularly acclaimed status as the "Peoples' Princess"—proclaimed by no less a personage than the Prime Minister himself—meant that the people would not countenance a private occasion. So it fell to the clergy of the Abbey, priests of the Church of England by law established, to devise a service that would serve. Some critical liturgical observers were quick to note that what emerged was not exactly the Office for the Burial of the Dead from the Book of Common Prayer or any of its authorized alternatives—but the service was not about Christian Burial: it was about Diana. Indeed, as one person observed, as Diana was "unique," so she required a "unique" service. It could not in the circumstances be otherwise. The religious elements were in place: the incomparable setting, the glorious music and the hymns, the solemn tolling of the Abbey bells, and even the presence of the body. As one of my English clerical colleagues observed, it was much like the modern memorial service, only with the body present. Hardly anyone remembers whatever it was that the Dean of Westminster said, but everyone remembers the rather self-serving remarks of the Earl Spencer, and the unavoidable presence of Elton John and his reworked elegy to Marilyn Monroe.

Tragedy, grief, melodrama, and the patent unfairness of celebrity death were very much the mood of that morning. Some have criticized the liturgy as "sub-Christian," which is to say, a minimalist concoction in which the hard facts of death, sin, and judgement were elided. In reviewing the tape of the proceedings I think this is a harsh judgement. Even if it was the case, it was only to give worldwide visibility to the sort of trimming that occurs daily in the crematoria and parish churches of England. It was considerably less "sub-Christian" than that other well-viewed funeral in the movie *Four Weddings and a Funeral*, which did so much for the literary estate of W. H. Auden.

Compare Diana's service to that for President Kennedy in 1963, when another nation was engulfed in grief for a life of promise and distinction untimely taken. The Mass at St. Matthew's Cathedral in Washington was still remorselessly pre-Vatican II, and was up to that point perhaps the most widely witnessed requiem in history. Two popular sentiments emerged from that occasion, particularly among Protestants not altogether used to the public ways of the Roman church. The first was, "Those Catholics certainly know how to deal with death"; and the second, to be heard, alas, all too frequently in the decades since, was, "Those Kennedys are remarkably sustained in their grief by their Catholic faith."

At the 1965 state funeral of Sir Winston Churchill in St. Paul's Cathedral, planned to the last detail by the great man himself, in addition to the singing of "The Battle Hymn of The Republic" as a gesture to his American mother, Jenny Jerome, and in an innovation worthy of the man and of the occasion, it was arranged to have a trumpeter sound "The Last Post," the English equivalent of "Taps," in the whispering gallery of the great dome. As its last notes died a trumpet responded on the other side of the dome with "Reveille." The symbolism, consistent with the rites celebrated below, could not be lost on anyone.

PERSPECTIVE AND PRIORITY

Religion is the business of coming to terms with death, and it is the certainty of death that gives order and opportunity for life. For Christians, all of our central liturgical activity has to do with coming to terms. Even in the rite of initiation which is baptism, the leading metaphor is the action whereby one is buried to sin, and hence is dead to sin, rising to newness of life. In the practice of baptism by immersion this figure is advanced by the physical "burial" into the waters which symbolize at the same time both the grave and the source of newness of life from which one rises. All other forms of baptism take the same principle, although it might be expressed differently.

In the Eucharist, the meal of thanksgiving or the Holy Communion, the body and blood are death redeemed. The Church Fathers called the holy meal holy or divine medicine that is the source of health and life *contra* sickness and death. Also, by the transaction of the Eucharist whether in memorial, consubstantiation, transubstantiation, or real presence, death is mitigated. It is the Easter action whereby, in the words of the medieval Easter hymn, the "death of death and hell's destruction" is reenacted.

When the intimate relationship between death and life is forgotten and the emphasis placed upon life, the great inevitability of death raises the question of the meaning, the value, and the worth of life itself. The existential crisis to which Paul Tillich spoke so powerfully in his book *The Courage To Be*, nearly fifty years ago, has to do with the sense of meaninglessness which death imposes upon life. "In the end we are all dead" is a statement not just of fact, but of despair as well. It is to confront and overcome that despair that the Christian faith upholds the defeat of death as its chief conviction. Despite the fact that the New Testament begins with the synoptic gospels and the "memoirs" of Jesus according to the four witnesses, the motivating principle of primitive or formative Christianity is neither the incarnation nor the atonement but the resurrection. Here nature and all that is presumed to be orderly and natural is turned on its head. Death, which is understood to be the natural end of all things, is now defined as an enemy to be overcome. St. Paul says as much when in I Corinthians 15:23 he writes, "The last enemy that shall be destroyed is death." It is Paul who argues that if it is alone for this life that Christians have hope, "we are of all men most miserable"; but that is no longer the case, he argues, for the resurrection of Jesus is not just a good ending for him, but a promise to all who believe. The risen Jesus has become "the first fruits of them that sleep," that is, he has set an example which all others shall follow. Thus, in the Pauline figure, the "sting of death," the fear not of its inevitability but of its ultimate finality, has been removed. The implication is not that we shall not die, but that we shall not fear death nor be intimidated by it.

This is Paul's heroic effort to break the human bondage to death and the meaninglessness it implies for life, and it is done not by denying death or its claims. This liberation is accomplished literally by putting death in its place, a place over which God has dominion. Death thus becomes the fixed point against which the quality of human life is measured, and the point of transition beyond which is to be found what, for lack of a better term, the Church calls "eternal life." Interestingly, Paul spends little time speculating on the nature of life beyond the grave. Unlike many successor Christian theologians who speculate on the furniture, geography, and temperature of the life and world to come, Paul spends his energy on how one ought to live on this side of death. In Colossians 3:1–4, 12–17, he says that the resurrection has a this-worldly ethical component that cannot be ignored, and must be embraced as proof of the resurrection's efficacy not only for Jesus in the past but for the faithful in the future. The context of that efficacy, however, is the immediate now. "If then you have been raised with Christ," he writes, "seek the things that are above, where Christ is seated at the right hand of God." In other words, there is a new standard of conduct and behavior in the world here and now as a result of the past and future resurrection. Those standards are high and demanding: "Put on then, as God's chosen ones, holy and beloved, compassion, kindness, lowliness, meekness, and patience, forbearing one another and, if one has a complaint against another, forgiving each other; as the Lord has forgiven you, so you also must forgive."

The ethical implications of the resurrection, alas, are not given the attention they deserve in much of our pastoral and theological speculation. Paul's ethics and those of the earliest Christians derive from the conviction that the "death of death," which is accomplished by Jesus in the resurrection, makes it possible for people to aspire to live before death in anticipation of the way life is to be lived after death. Because death is not the end, which would make life—no matter how well lived—meaningless, life is now to be lived free of the intimidations of death, and meaning is derived both from aspiration to a human imitation of the divine example, and a divine judgement of the effort.

Another element that adds to the human impetus to be and to do good is the comparison of the shortness and uncertainty of human life, and the eternal definiteness of the life of God. The Book of Common Prayer puts it this way:

> O God, whose days are without end, and whose mercies cannot be numbered: make us, we pray, deeply aware of the shortness and uncertainty of human life; and let your Holy Spirit lead us in holiness and righteousness all our days; that, when we shall have served you in our generation, we may be gathered to our ancestors, having the testimony of a good conscience, in the communion of the Catholic Church, in the confidence of a certain faith, in the comfort of a religious and holy hope, in favor with you, our God, and in perfect charity with the world.

BREAKING THE SILENCE

The phrase "the good life" has a frustrating ambiguity about it. It once meant a life beyond reproach in which one lived "in favor with you, our God, and in perfect charity with the world." It was that toward which our ethics, values, and morals pointed. The good life was the work of a lifetime. There is, however, another meaning to the phrase "the good life," which in our material and secular parlance means full access to the good things of this world: pleasure, delight, and, indeed, the constitutionally guaranteed right to the pursuit of happiness.

In the first construction of the "good life," the reward or consequence was what pastoral theology calls the "good death," a death which finds the believer reconciled with God, neighbor, and self, unafraid and content. In the second construction, death is the spoiler and the intruder, the unbidden and unwelcome guest, the ironic and inevitable end to a life of apparent immortality. Because in this construction of the "good life" death is ignored, death comes as a nasty and arbitrary surprise for which there has been no preparation, either cultural or existential. The good death and this particular good life are in irresolvable conflict. Michael Ignatieff puts it this way:

> However blind life or the spiral may be, there is an hour when it all stops. . . . What then will we need? We no longer share a vision of the good death. Most other cultures, including many primitive ones whom we have subjugated to our reason and our technology, enfold their members in an art of dying as in an art of living. But we have left these awesome tasks of culture to private choice. . . . We have created a new need, the need to live an examined life; we pursue its satisfaction in the full babble of conflicting opinions about what life is for, and we pursue it in a collectively held silence about the meaning of death.[2]

The one place where there is not meant to be a "silence about the meaning of death" is in the Christian church. Its resources to speak to this subject are extraordinary, but in subjugation or captivity to the death-denying popular culture in which it finds itself, the church often colludes in the euphemization of death. We no longer "bury the dead"; instead, we hold services for the "celebration of life." There is no longer a "sting" in death, as Paul put it, but it has become a "blessed release," or a "sweet mercy." In the medical world, by which we are increasingly governed, death is regarded as the ultimate defeat, or worse, failure. The doctors withdraw and go to fight more winnable battles, leaving the nurses, the family, and the clergy, when present, to cope with imminent death. The silence is deafening.

I used to think that the funerary customs of my youth were barbaric and sentimental: the wake, the mourning bands and wreaths, the open casket, the lowering away of the coffin into the grave in the presence of the mourners, the seasons of mourning, and so forth. I know the arguments for the alterations in all of these customs, most of which are meant to lift the heavy presence of death from the bereaved, for it is somehow society's purpose to get the bereaved "over it" as quickly as possible, and in fact not to mention "it" at all. Thus it is the bereaved who embarrass us by talking about "it" all of the time. Public and inconsolable grief is modernity's greatest and last taboo, as it reminds us all of how vulnerable and fragile we are and that even caregivers and grief therapists will eventually die. The mourner is somehow not simply a reminder of the dead, but a rebuke to the living.

If the old cliche to "hang a lantern on your problem" has any truth to it, perhaps we could learn from our ancestors how to conquer the silence about death and recover the art of dying as a part of the art of living. This was once considered the first and central work of the church, and perhaps it can become so once again. Few theological schools offer courses in "The Theology of Death," or "Death and Pastoral Care"; and few preaching courses encourage would-be preachers to preach regularly to their people on the notion of the good death and the relationship between death and life in Christian belief, apart from the particular occasions of death, and not always then. The Victorians were accused, with some justification, of the romanticization of death. We moderns, however, with equal justice, may be charged with the sanitization of death, in collusion with the practitioners of what is now called "mortuary science."

If we are to recover the sense of death as an inevitable part of life, and to make the connection between the good life and the good death as twin goals to which we aspire, we will have to recover a language and reappropriate symbols with which to speak of death and dying within the context of living and meaning. For the religious community, and for its ministers and priests in particular, this will mean reaffirming the principle that religion has as among its chief objectives teaching us how to live so that we may come to terms with death. This does not invite speculation about the life to come, despite the vivid examples of such speculation with which Christian theology is littered. We need only remember the Bible's reticence in that speculation. One thing about which the Bible is clear, however, is, as Paul puts it in Romans 14:8, "If we live, we live to the Lord, and if we die, we die to the Lord; so then, whether we live or whether we die, we are the Lord's." For the believer it is essential to be reminded over and over again that the Lord's claims upon us are not abrogated by death, and hence both how we live and how we die are encompassed by our faithfulness to God, and God's faithfulness to us. Life is the context in which faith reminds us of that fact.

NOTES

1. John Henry Newman, *Watching*.
2. Michael Ignatieff.

Is There Life after Death?

JÜRGEN MOLTMANN

I. IS DEATH THE END? IS THERE LIFE AFTER DEATH? WHY DO WE ASK? WHAT ARE WE ASKING ABOUT?

What remains of our lives when we die? That is the question we ask when we pause in the midst of life's "ever-rolling stream" and search for the thing that sustains us. Where are the dead? We ask about their future when we stand at the grave of someone we love, and when we mourn the people who were the joy of our lives; for when they die, our love of life dies too. So where are we going? Do we await anything? What awaits us?

What lasts? Does anything last at all? Of course we are overwhelmed by this question when we feel the cold breath of death—our own death, or the death of people we love. When people are in the grip of a serious illness we say that they are fighting for their lives. If they win, life is given back to them and they are as if newborn; if they lose, they vanish away, like all the other things that once made their lives what they were. Death seems to us final—the end—gone—nevermore.

But we ask about death not just at the end of someone's life. The question is always with us. It is the question about time; for "our days are soon gone and we fly away," as Psalm 90 laments. We cannot hold onto a single moment, even if, like Goethe's Faust, we long to say: "O tarry a while, thou art so fair." For we ourselves cannot tarry. The lived moment passes, and we pass away, too, "in the twinkling of an eye." Nothing remains, for time is irreversible and what has once become the past can never be brought back. The future we hope for and work for will, if our hopes for it are fulfilled, become our present, and our expectations will then become the experiences we longed for. But every present passes, and what is past never returns. Expectations become experiences, and experiences turn into remembrances, and

53

remembrances will in the end become the great forgetting which we call death. Yet something in us rises up in protest: "Is that all this life has to offer?"

When we ask about a life after death we are always asking at the same time about a meaningful, livable, and loved life before death. For what could a life after death mean for us unless there can be a fulfilled life before death which we affirm?

II. WHAT REMAINS OF LIFE?

We are familiar with very old religious ideas expressed in the pictures of early peoples, where the immortal soul of a human being is shown departing from the body after death, leaving that body behind as a lifeless corpse, while the soul returns to its eternal home in a heaven beyond earth. The ancient Egyptians imagined the soul as a bird, with the human face of the dead person, and Elisabeth Kübler-Ross found a striking number of butterflies in the pictures painted by children in Auschwitz. In medieval pictures, the soul enters the body before birth in the form of a tiny human being with angel's wings, so that after the person's death it can fly away and return to heaven. Obituary notices often cite a famous verse written by Eichendorff:

> And so my soul
> Spread wide her wings,
> Flew through the silent lands
> As if she flew towards home.

That is a lovely picture even though the "as if" in the last line suggests a romantic unreality. Every prisoner knows the longing which the free flight of a bird awakens, the longing for "the broad place in which there is no cramping."

But what do we mean when we talk about the soul as the part of our life that is immortal? Do we mean the immortality of the unlived life, or the immortality of the lived life?

According to our Western philosophical tradition, which goes back to Plato, the human soul is essentially and in substance immortal. Death does not kill it. Death merely divides the immortal soul from the mortal body, which then lies there, a lifeless corpse. For all those who loved that body, with its senses and passions, death may be a reason for

grief. But for the soul, death is the greatest feast day on the way to freedom in its own world of Ideas. Because it is immortal, it only occupied
this mortal body as a guest, or as if in a prison.

Why is the soul immortal, while everything else in us is, after all,
mortal? The answer is a simple one, even if it is not universally familiar: the soul cannot die because it was never born. Because it was there
before the child's birth, it will still be there after the old man or woman
has died. Its life after death is its life before birth as well; for its "eternal life" is beyond the birth and death of this life. But if the soul is never
born and cannot die, it has nothing in common with the physical, sensory world of this life of birth and mortality. It is in its substance immutable, always the same, incapable of suffering and hence incapable
of happiness too. In the sense of what we call life, or "livingness," the
soul is lifeless. To put it epigrammatically, what is meant by the immortal soul is not the immortality of the lived life; it is the immortality
of the life that has never lived. But if that is true, then this doctrine of
the immortal soul offers us no answer to the question: What remains
of life? And yet the consciousness of "possessing" an immortal soul
gives people serenity and imperturbability in the ups and downs of life,
and makes them indifferent toward life and death. Self-transcendence
and the self-irony which prevents one from taking oneself too seriously:
those are their virtues. We find this not merely in the philosophy of the
Greek Stoics, but in the Indian *Bhagavad Gītā* as well.

> It is neither born nor does it die,
> as it once was, so it remains,
> unborn, immortal.

> He who is steadfast in joy and pain,
> remains himself at every hour,
> ripens for immortality.

> He who renounces all desire,
> from selfishness and longing free
> walking this earth,
> he enters into tranquil peace.
> (2:15–17)

But when we talk about the soul today, do we really mean these
attributes of untouchability? When we talk about an "ensouled life,"
we mean the wholly and entirely living life, not the life that is unlived.

We mean a life that is open, capable of happiness and capable of suffering, a life full of love. If we say that a mother is "the soul of her family," we certainly do not mean that she is the part of the family which nothing can touch. We mean that she keeps her family together, and makes it a living entity. So I understand "the soul" in a different way from Plato. Human life is entirely human when it is entirely living. But human livingness means being interested in life, participating and communicating, and affirming one's own life and the life of others. This vital interest is what we call love of life. It expresses itself in a life that is wholly and completely lived because it is a life that is loved. Our "soul" is present when we give ourselves up to something completely, are passionately interested, and—because love makes us strong—do not hold life back but move out from ourselves. But if we move out from ourselves we become capable of love, and also capable of suffering. We experience the livingness of life—and at the same time the deadliness of death. But how can we really give ourselves up to this life, with its conflicts, its happiness, and its disappointments and pains, if we do not put more confidence in this love for life than in transient time and death? The real human problem is not the dualism of an immortal soul and a mortal body; it is the conflict between love and death.

Can this loved, ensouled, and mortal life be immortal? This obvious contradiction is resolved if, instead of ascribing immortality to a substance like the Platonic soul, we see it as a relationship of the whole person to the immortal God. Ever since its beginnings, Christian theology has worked on this transformation of the idea of immortality. Let me mention some different stages and aspects.

a) In both the Old and New Testaments, immortality is always postulated of the divine Spirit (*ruach, pneuma*) which gives life to us and to all the living. "Into thy hands I commend my spirit," prays the dying Jesus according to Luke (23:46), using the words of Psalm 31:6, the Jewish evening prayer. Christian poets have taken up this idea. One hymn writer calls the Spirit "the seal of immortality." Another writes:

> Breathe on me, Breath of God,
> So shall I never die,
> But live with Thee the perfect life
> Of thine eternity.[1]

According to biblical ideas, this Spirit, who is the giver of life (*spiritus vivificans*), is a divine relationship out of which life and the blessing of life proceed. What divine relationship?

b) Human beings are created to be the image of God on earth. That is to say, God puts himself in relationship to these created beings in such a way that they become his mirror and reflection, and the response to him. If God is God, his relation to his human image cannot be destroyed, either through the antagonism and recalcitrance of human beings or through their death. Only God himself could dissolve the relationship to his creatures into which he has entered, if he were to "be sorry" he created them, as the story about Noah and the Flood tells. But as long as God holds fast to this relationship to human beings, to be made in the image of God remains the inalienable and indestructible destiny of human beings. If this were not so, the powers of time and death would be mightier than God. For human beings, what results from the special relation of God to them is called life, soul, or "spirit."

c) This certainly does not mean "spirit" in the sense in which we often use the word. The Hebrew word *ruach* means the energy and force of life. It fills the whole lived life, which means a person's whole life history from birth to death, everything we mean when we use a person's name.

"Fear not, for I have redeemed you; I have called you by your name, you are mine." So we say in the words of Isa. 43:1, at a sickbed or standing before a grave. But what is meant by a person's name? Surely not just that person's disembodied soul or soulless body, but rather the whole configuration of the person's life in space, and the whole history of his or her life in time. If this living configuration is called by name, then as a consequence our whole life becomes immortal in God's relation to it. As mortal, transitory men and women, in the immortal and intransient fellowship with God we ourselves remain immortal and intransient. How can we conceive of this?

d) The American process theology of Alfred North Whitehead and Charles Hartshorne calls this remaining in relationship to God *objective immortality*. It is not just that God affects everything; everything has its effect on God too. People are not just created by God. They themselves, for their part, also make an impression on God. It is not just we who experience God. God "experiences" us too. The "experience" which God has of us remains existent in him even when we die. Our life in time is transitory, but we have an eternal presence in God. The history of our lives is fleeting. We ourselves forget quickly. But for God that life history is like a book of life in which his experience of our lives remains eternally in his memory. This idea about an objective immortality in God's eternity is still not in itself a consoling idea. Would we really like to be reminded to all eternity of everything we have ever said, done, and experienced? But according to the psalms in the Old Testament, God's memory is not a video of our lives, recorded from heaven and played back to all eternity. It is a merciful, healing remembrance, which puts things to rights. "Remember me according to thy mercy,"[2] and "remember not the sins of my youth."[3] It is the shining countenance of God's love which looks at us, not the cold, impersonal lens of a monitor set up by a state security authority.

e) God's relation to human beings which makes these human beings come alive is also termed *dialogical immortality*. "The one to whom God speaks, whether in wrath or in grace, that one is surely immortal," said Luther. This idea has the support of many theologians. People remain God's conversation partner, even if they do not listen. Even death cannot alter that. But if they do listen, their whole life becomes a responsive existence. They respond, and make themselves responsible. If that is correct, then death is the boundary of our lives, but not the boundary of God's relationship to us. In that relationship, our death is rather a gateway or connecting door, a transformation on our side. The speaking, calling, and ultimately redeeming relationship of God to us endures.

f) Finally, there is in faith an experience of fellowship with Christ which leads to a *subjective immortality*, and a positive hope of resurrection. This is the experience of being in the divine Spirit a child of God's. "All who are led by the Spirit of God are children of God," says Paul. As God's children, they belong to God's family and lineage, and by virtue of hope already participate here and now in the eternal life of God's future world. In the Spirit of the resurrection, they already, here and now, experience that eternal life as eternal livingness in love.

So let us sum up: What remains of life?

We have two impressions. On the one hand we cannot hold fast to anything, not even ourselves. Everything passes; naked we came into the world; naked we shall leave it. Death is the finish.

But on the other hand nothing is lost at all. Everything remains in God. Before God, with God, and in God we mortal beings are immortal, and our transitory life remains—intransitory. Our life as we experience it is temporal and mortal. But as God experiences our life it remains eternally immortal. Nothing is lost with God, not the moments of happiness, not the times of pain. "All live to him" (Luke 20:38).

III. WHERE ARE THE DEAD?

"Where are the dead?" sounds like a speculative question, but that is not the case. Where do we really experience death? At the end of my own life what I experience is dying but not death, because I do not survive my death on earth. But when the people I love die, I experience their death, for I have to survive that death, mourn their loss, and go on living in spite of it. Life is good, but to be a survivor is hard. This means that what we experience ourselves is dying, but in other people we experience death. The question "Where are the dead?" is a momentous question for us personally, because it is a question about the community of the living with the dead, and is important for a life in their presence.

I remember what was for me a painfully embarrassing situation. Ernst Bloch had just died. He was a neighbor of ours, and I went over at once to speak to his wife. She came toward me and simply asked: "Where is he now?" His body was still in the house. For the moment I was without an answer. But I have learned that this "where" question is important for the people left behind, because without an answer they cannot hold fast to fellowship with the "beloved person" (as Bloch's wife called her Ernst).

Let us now look at three ideas about the life of the dead, submitting them to a critical question: Do they strengthen the love of the living for the dead?

a) The doctrine of purgatory. This is unknown in Protestant circles and among people without any church connections. (In an examination, one Protestant theological student answered my question about purgatory by saying that he supposed it was hell for Catholics.) The dogmatic starting point for the development of the idea of purgatory can be found in a declaration made in 1336 by Pope Benedict XII. He rejected the idea that the dead sleep until the resurrection at the Last Day. After their own personal death, Michael Schmaus explained, everyone is immediately judged, confronted by God with the whole truth about the life they have lived, in the light of what they themselves know; they become their own judge. Many people have experienced something like this in near-death situations: their whole life passes before them in quick motion, in a flash. If someone dies in faith in Christ, his or her sins are certainly forgiven, but the consequences of sin remain. They have not yet been expiated through temporal punishments.

Life before death is a continual repentance, and life after death is continued as a similar process of purgation and purification. This process is purgatory. It has nothing to do with hell; on the contrary. To put it in modern terms, in death the believing soul experiences the presence of God as light and fire. The light of the eternal love draws it to God; the fire of eternal love burns away everything which is in opposition to God, and which cuts the soul off from him. Some people who have stood at the threshold of death tell of visions of light and fire like this. The basic idea of the doctrine of purgatory can be found in Christ's promise that "the pure in heart shall see God" (Matt. 5:8). Consequently the purification of the heart must be continued until the contemplation of God can take place—the *visio beatifico*, or beatific vision.

In the world of religious ideas, heaven and hell are terminuses, the end of the road. But the idea of purgatory permits God's history with a person to continue after death. That is why Dante writes in his *Divine Comedy* (1319): "Beloved son, let thy hope rise," whereas over the gates to hell are written the words: "Abandon hope, all ye who enter here." In Dante, purgatory lies on a mountain of purification, with seven stages, a mountain which reaches from earth up to heaven.

Can the living do anything for the "poor souls in purgatory"? A tenet of faith says that in Christ the living and the dead are a great communion—a "penitential community." So if someone acquires an indulgence—a remission of the punishment for his or her sins—that person has the right to ask God to pass on to the dead the remission of punishment that has been granted. But the most efficacious help is the Mass for the dead.

Protestant criticism of the notion of purgatory is familiar. As we all know, the Reformation began with Luther's attack on Tetzel's trade in indulgences, an advertising slogan for which has come down to us: "The moment that the money rings, the soul from purgatory springs." In the Smalcald Articles, Luther criticized the "fair-ground trafficking in purgatorial Masses"; and Calvin called purgatory "a pernicious invention of Satan." Both Luther and Calvin proclaimed that what Christ has done is sufficient for all our sins, so there is no need for the souls of the dead to perform anything additional for their salvation by enduring punishment. But with their criticism the Reformers were attacking only the concept of penance and the "penitential community of the living and the dead." They were not criticizing—though they were not of course aware of the fact—the idea that God's history with human beings continues after death. Nor were they calling in question the community of the living and the dead in Christ.

b) A second idea, which we find in Luther and in modern Catholic theology, is the doctrine of the soul's sleep or resurrection at death. Luther conceived the state of the dead as a deep, dreamless sleep, removed from time and space, without consciousness and without feeling. In this concept he did not think so much from here to there, as from there to here. When the dead are raised by Christ "on the Last Day," they will know neither how long they have slept nor where they are. We shall rise "suddenly" and shall not know how we came to die, or how we have passed through death.

> As soon as thy eyes have closed shalt thou be woken, a thousand years shall be as if thou hadst slept but a little half hour. Just as at night we hear the clock strike and know not how long we have slept, so too, and how much more, are in death a thousand years soon past. Before a man should turn round, he is already a fair angel.[4]

The theological reasoning is as follows:

> Because before God's face time is not counted, a thousand years before Him must be as it were but a single day. Hence the first man Adam is as close to Him as will be the last to be born before the final Day. For God seeth time, not according to its length but athwart it, transversely. Before God all hath happened at once.[5]

When Luther calls death a sleep, this does not mean that he is drawing a veil over the brute fact of death. What he means is, first, that death has lost its power over human beings, and, second, that it is not the last thing which awaits us. Both affirmations presuppose Christ's resurrection from the dead, for with that, death surrendered its power to Christ. It still has its "form," as Luther says, but no longer its power.

How long does the soul's sleep last—what the hymn calls "death's dark night"? Luther does not reply with projections drawn from the time of the living and extrapolated onto a continued existence of the soul. He finds expressions for God's time: "suddenly, in a moment." The Last Day is "the Day of the Lord," so it is not just the last day; it is the "day of days," the time of the eternal present. How long will it be from the hour of our own death until the dead are raised into the eternal kingdom? Just "an instant." Where are the dead now, in terms of our time? They are already in the world of the resurrection. "Today," not "in three days," not "at the Last Day," but *today* you will be with me in Paradise," says the dying Christ to the man dying on the cross beside him (Luke 23:43, emphasis added).

Karl Rahner and other Catholic theologians have taken up this idea about "resurrection at death." The ecumenical *New Book of Belief* of 1973 (*Das Neue Glaubensbuch*) says: "Individual resurrection from the dead takes place with and at death." Unfortunately, in his first declaration as cardinal, Joseph Ratzinger, through the medium of the Congregation for the Doctrine of the Faith, rejected this idea, for it makes indulgences and Masses for the dead superfluous, and therefore runs counter to the practice of the Church.

c) This brings us to the much discussed question about possible reincarnations. Do we live only once on this earth, or are we reborn many times?

Although a soul which cannot die cannot be born either, from time immemorial the notion of an immortal soul has often been linked with ideas about the transmigration of souls, and their reincarnation in new forms of life. Everything that lives comes into being and passes away. Why should it not come into being again afresh? If we cease to look at our own lives, but consider life's great cohesions in the community of human beings and the community shared by all the living, then the notion of the eternal return appears quite normal, and the idea that a life is unique and original seems actually something out of the way. Plato and Plotinus, Lessing and Goethe particularly were attracted to the doctrine of reincarnation, and the New Age movement has taken it up as well.

First, every doctrine of reincarnation sets the individual life in the wider community of the generations and of all the living. All are related to all others. Do not kill an animal—it might harbor your mother's soul! Do no living thing an injustice—in the next life you could be that same living thing! If we see the souls of human beings, animals, and plants within the great cohesion of the world soul, then all live together in an ensouled cosmos. The Abrahamic religions, in contrast, have linked their conviction about the counterpart of a personal God with a belief in the uniqueness of the human person, and the individual life which can never be brought back. People are not just "part of nature" (as the United Nations Earth Charter says). They are an image of the invisible God too. In this relationship to God they are above the patterns and cohesions of nature. Before God, every person is an original, not a replica, and God never clones. From this follows the respect for the individuality of every life, and the uniqueness of the lived moment.

From the biblical standpoint, those who believe in reincarnation must be asked whether their doctrine does not very considerably reduce the number of existing souls. Surely the claim to have already lived several times, or to have been reborn again and again, means a tremendous ousting of other people from their own lives? I remember seeing the film in which a Tibetan Lama dies, and the monks look for the reincarnation of his soul. They find it in a little Chinese boy, and revere him accordingly. The boy can no longer live his own life, for he is no longer himself.

From the standpoint of the doctrines of reincarnation, the Abrahamic religions must in their turn be asked whether the personal elevation of human beings above nature, with its warp and woof, does not destroy the community of the living on earth, and whether it is not responsible for the ecological catastrophes of the modern world. That leads us to a synthesis: as persons before God, people are part of nature; and as part of nature they are persons before God. Their unique character as the image of God does not cut them off from nature, but merely describes their particular task within nature. Persons are not individuals. They are social beings, and live in community with each other, in the community of the generations and in the community of creation. It is quite possible to mediate fruitfully between the Western understanding of person and the Eastern understanding of nature— not only possible, but virtually necessary. The critical questions lie elsewhere.

Second, every doctrine of reincarnation is faced with the question of how it can hold fast to the soul's identity in the transmigrations into the forms of life which that soul assumes. If I am reborn as a human being, I must be able to preserve my soul's human identity. If I am reborn as an animal, or if I once died as a tree, this identity cannot be preserved. It passes away with the human form of my life. If I have the impression that "I have been here before," I must be able to recognize myself in that past form of life. My *I* or self cannot be mortal.

But if my *I* is part of this life, I shall not be able to recognize myself again, however often I am reborn. And according to ancient Indian teaching, the soul does not really "migrate." The *Bhagavad Gita* says:

> As a man casts off his worn-out clothes
> and takes on other new ones,
> So does the embodied self cast off
> its worn-out bodies and enter new ones. (2:22)

But if the soul is without individuality, it is not a determining subject that can migrate or change its clothing. So in Buddhism the idea of a "transmigration of souls without a soul" was thought through further:

> Is the one who is born again the same as the one who departs, or different? Neither the same nor another. . . . One appearance emerges, another disappears, yet they all range themselves to each other without interruption. In this way the final constitution of the consciousness is attained neither as the same person nor as another. (*Milinda Panha*)

That is a typical Asian "neither/nor" in place of the "either/or" of Western thinking.

Third, according to ancient Indian teaching, the reincarnations belong to the wheel of rebirth; and according to the teaching about karma, they are the requital for good and evil acts in a former life. They are the materialized consequences of sin, so to speak. According to Western Spiritism and New Age teaching, they belong to the evolutionary principle of the modern world. The doctrine of karma maintains that there is an inexorable and inescapable link between act and destiny: "The person who steals corn will become a rat" (and "You have made your bed; now lie in it"). No power in the world can break this link, and no God either. But in the Western interpretation, reincarnations are supposed to give us "a second chance," so that we can do better next time, as Elisabeth Kübler-Ross believes. "Little by little we climb higher and higher up the ladder of progress until we reach the stages of perfection," taught the Spiritist Alan Kardec. There is thus a contradiction between the Eastern and the Western judgement of reincarnation; for the one it is retribution, for the other a chance.

The biblical religions recognized a type of karma too, one which spans generations: "The fathers have eaten sour grapes, and the children's teeth are set on edge."[6] This is proverbial wisdom: "He who sows the wind will reap the whirlwind."[7] But what is special and new in the biblical traditions is the principle of grace, which breaks through the general chain linking act and destiny, setting it aside and invalidating it: "His grace is new every morning."[8] "He who forgives all your sins and heals your infirmities"[9] is himself the power of life which breaks through the laws of karma and destiny, and replaces retribution with a new beginning.

Finally, this also means that the cosmic law of karma cannot be pressed into service to explain the disabilities, illnesses, or sufferings of the present, tracing them back to the guilt of the sufferer's forbears. The dead of Auschwitz: what karmic guilt are they supposed to have expiated? The dead of Hiroshima: what karmic retribution are they supposed to have suffered?

III. THE FUTURE OF THE SPOILED AND CURTAILED LIFE

Much in our lives remains unfinished. We began something, but did not carry it through to the end. We tried to make a plan for our lives but the plan was spoiled. Life was promised us, and the promise remained unfulfilled. How can a life here ever be "complete" or "successful"? However we may imagine eternal death or eternal life, it can surely not mean the eternalization of our unsuccessful beginnings or miscarried attempts at life. It is impressions of this kind which make us think about an ongoing history of God's with our lived lives and which give us the feeling that the dead are still not at rest. Whether the idea be purgatory or the transmigration of souls, the feeling remains: I must or shall again come back to this life so as to set right the things that have gone wrong, pay off the debts, heal the pains, and complete what was never completed.

But it is not just the harsh caesuras in the story of our own lives which make us ask about a life after death. I think of the life of those who were unable to live and were not allowed to live: the beloved child dying at birth; the little boy run over when he was four; the sixteen-year-old friend torn to pieces by a bomb as he stood beside me, a bomb which left me unscathed—and all the many people who have been raped and murdered and exterminated. Of course their fate can be of great importance for other people, but where will their own lives be "completed"? Where and how will they find "rest"?

The idea that for these people their death is the end would surely plunge the whole world into absolute absurdity; for if their lives had no meaning, has ours? The modern notion about a "natural death" may be appropriate enough for members of the affluent society, with their life insurance, who can afford a death in old age. But in the countries of the Third World most people die a premature, violent, and by no means affirmed death, like so many people of my generation, who died in the Second World War. The idea of an "eternalization of the lived life" does not take in the people who were not able to live or were not permitted to do so. So do we not have to think the thought of an ongoing history of God's with the spoiled and curtailed life, if we are to be able to affirm life in this ravaged world, and to love it in spite of all its cruelties?

I believe that God will also complete the work which he has begun with a human life. If God is God, even violent death cannot stop him from doing so. So I believe that God's history with our lives will go on after our deaths, until that completion has been reached in which a soul finds rest. According to theological tradition, this is not as yet "the kingdom of God," nor is it yet "the life of the world to come"; it is a kind of intermediate state between the life that has died here and eternal life there. An intermediate state of this kind is presupposed by the doctrines of purgatory and reincarnation, but the idea of a great divine judgement also gives a name to something between our death and eternal life. I do not believe in the necessary performance of penitential acts in a purgatory. Nor do I believe in a great and final divine criminal court of justice. For me, God's judgement means the final putting to rights of the injustice that has been done and suffered, and the final raising up of those who are bowed down. So I conceive of that intermediate state as a wide space for living, in which the life which was spoiled and cut short here can develop freely. I imagine it as the time of a new life, in which God's history with a human being can come to its flowering and consummation. I imagine that we then come close to that well of life from which we could already here and now draw the power to live and the affirmation of life, so that the handicapped and the broken can live the life that was meant for them, for which they were born, and which was taken from them.

For that reason I do not believe either that we ought to compare that life with a sleep, as Luther did. We should rather, like Calvin, think of a great "waking and watching of the soul" after death, with which it "perceives" its healing and its completion, and "experiences" its rebirth for the life of the future world. Those whom we call the dead are not lost. But they are not yet finally saved either. Together with us who are still alive, they are hidden, sheltered, in the same hope, and are hence together with us on the way to God's future. They "watch" with us, and we "watch" with them. That is the community of hope shared by the dead with the living, and by the living with the dead.

I think all this not for selfish reasons, neither for the sake of a personal completion, nor in the interests of a moral purification, but for the sake of the justice which I believe is God's own concern and his first option.

NOTES

1. Edwin Hatch, "Breathe on Me, Breath of God."
2. Ps. 25:7.
3. Ibid.
4. Luther, *WA* 37.191.
5. Luther, *WA* 36.340.
6. Jer. 31:29.
7. Hos. 8:7
8. Lam. 3:23.
9. Ps. 103:3.

PART II

Death and Immortality in Various Cultures

If I Should Die before
I Am Awakened:
Buddhist Reflections on Death

MALCOLM DAVID ECKEL

THE PRAYER THAT begins with the words "If I should die before I wake" comes from a slim but once ubiquitous volume known as *The New England Primer*.[1] This book helped generations of New England school children learn to read. It also introduced them to some of the hopes and fears of the New England Protestant heart, as is clear in one of the most prominent features in the eighteenth-century editions of the *Primer*, an exhortation written by Mr. John Rogers for his children before he was burned at the stake. The exhortation begins in the following way:

> Give ear my Children to my words,
> Whom God hath dearly bought,
> Lay up his Laws within your heart,
> And print them in your thought.
> I leave you here a little book,
> For you to look upon,
> That you may see your Father's face,
> When he is dead and gone. . . .
> To you my heirs of earthly Things,
> Which I do leave behind,
> That you may read and understand,
> And keep it in your mind.
> That as you have been Heirs of this
> Which once shall wear away,
> You also may possess that part,
> Which never shall decay.[2]

The core of the *Primer* consisted of short illustrations of the letters of
the alphabet beginning with A for Adam: "In Adam's Fall We Sinned
all." As theological fashions changed, the illustrations also changed. At
a certain point in its development, the text was evangelized with the
addition of biblical references. At other times the text was purged of
biblical references. Death remained a constant presence, however,
even in the book's most secular editions. In the edition of 1762, G was
for Glass: "As runs the Glass, our Life doth pass." Y was for Youth:
"While youth do chear, death may be near." And X was for Xerxes:
"Xerxes did die, and so must I."

In this fragile world, it was considered prudent to use the precious moments of wakefulness to guard against the perils of death:

> First in the Morning, when thou dost awake,
> To God for his Grace thy Petition make,
> Some Heavenly Petition use daily to say,
> That the God of Heaven may bless thee alway.

Thoughts of sleep brought thoughts of death:

> Awake, arise, behold thou hast
> Thy Life a Leaf, thy Breath a Blast;
> At Night lye down prepared to have
> Thy sleep, thy death, thy bed, thy grave.

But thoughts of sleep also brought thoughts of a metaphorical awakening—not just thoughts of a sleepy child shaking the cobwebs from
his or her head and setting off to school, but an awakening of con-
science, wary of death and conscious of grace.

> I in the Burying Place may see
> Graves shorter there than I;
> From Death's Arrest no Age is free,
> Young Children too may die;
> My God, may such an awful Sight,
> Awakening be to me!
> Oh! That by early Grace I might
> For Death prepared be.

How deeply the sensibility of the *Primer* penetrated children's imagi-
nations in the eighteenth and nineteenth centuries is a question best

left to American historians,[3] but it certainly infuses the prayer that gave the title for this book. When those of us who experienced some version of a traditional New England childhood gathered ourselves at the edge of the bed and prattled "Now I lay me down to sleep" as if it were all one word,[4] we placed ourselves in the world of the *Primer*: it was a child's world, balanced between a fear of death and a hope for awakening, where death and awakening or fear and hope seemed to be two sides of the same perilous religious state of mind.

There is no exact counterpart to *The New England Primer* in the Buddhist traditions of South and Southeast Asia, but Buddhists do have a rich tradition of storytelling for children. Looking back on her childhood in Sri Lanka, Ranjini Obeyesekere wrote: "I realize we were never given religious instruction as such, either in school or at home. We participated in Buddhist rituals and ceremonies, mostly with the extended kin group, went to temple on full moon days (that, too, mainly during vacations), and listened to many, many Buddhist stories. That was how we learned to be Buddhists."[5] Many of these stories came from the body of literature known as the *Jātaka* or "birth" *Tales* about the previous lives of the Buddha.[6] To have a sequence of lives, of course, you have to have a sequence of deaths. Birth and death are part of the same package. One invariably follows the other until there is a Buddha who can bring the cycle to an end. It is not surprising to discover that many of the *Jātaka Tales* revolve around a crisis of death.

There is a famous *Jātaka Tale* about the bodhisattva (or "future Buddha") as the "king" of a herd of deer.[7] According to the story, Brahmadatta, the king of Benares, loved to hunt and in his hunting laid waste to a herd of deer. The bodhisattva, as the leader of the herd, approached the king and negotiated a deal: if the king stopped attacking the herd, one of the deer would offer itself for the king's table every day. The agreement worked for a while until the lot fell to a pregnant doe. She pleaded with the rest of the herd to protect her fawn by finding another deer to take her place. When none volunteered, the bodhisattva offered to sacrifice himself. The text tells us that he made a handsome and impressive sight as he walked up to the door of the palace and presented himself to the king. The king asked why such an extraordinary creature would present himself willingly for death. The king was so impressed by the explanation and by the inherent nobility of the deer that he promised to protect the lives not only of the deer,

but of all the living creatures in his kingdom. The king's promise reso-
nates with the language of Buddhist renunciation: "This deer is
renouncing himself (*ātmānam parityajati*) for someone else. He un-
derstands the Dharma in a way that we do not. . . . I will give him and
the herd the gift of fearlessness."

For a young person who wanted to follow the example of the
bodhisattva and become a Buddha, no story was more important than
the story of the future Buddha's renunciation. In his last birth, the
bodhisattva was born as Siddhārtha Gautama to a princely family in a
region of India that is now located in southern Nepal. According to
Buddhist legends, Siddhārtha Gautama was raised in luxury and insu-
lated from the ordinary sufferings of life. He married, had a child, and
then, in his early thirties, saw four troubling sights: a sick man, an old
man, a corpse, and a wandering monk. The sights left him shaken. He
realized that life was fleeting and full of pain, and he decided to become a wandering monk to find a solution to the problems of suffering, old age, and death. In the middle of the night when the rest of the
palace was asleep, Siddhārtha Gautama went forth from the palace,
cut off his hair, gave up his possessions, and began a life of strict self-
discipline and meditation. The solution he was looking for came to him
in a moment that is called his "awakening" (*bodhi*)—the event that
made him a Buddha—and he spent the rest of his life teaching, consoling, and presiding over a growing band of disciples who chose to follow his example.

What kind of a solution did the Buddha discover? To answer this
question in a Buddhist way requires some understanding of the traditional Indian approach to the meaning of death. Several centuries before the time of the Buddha, Indian people had come to think that
death was not something that happened once and for all. It happened
again and again as a person died and was reborn in a process known
as *saṃsāra*, or the "wandering" of a soul from one life to the next. In
English we are accustomed to calling this process "reincarnation" or
"rebirth," but it is more faithful to the Indian tradition to call it "re-
death." The challenge for a sage like the Buddha was to find a way
through the forest of *saṃsāra* so that a person could die in peace and
never be reborn. The way that the Buddha found is called the Noble
Eightfold Path (consisting of right understanding, right thought, right
speech, right action, right livelihood, right effort, right mindfulness,

and right concentration), and the goal of the path is called nirvana, the cessation of suffering and desire and the blissful termination of the process of rebirth.

The formulaic phrases of Buddhist doctrine do little justice, however, to the depth and seriousness of Buddhist approaches to death. Like other religious traditions, Buddhism brings these concepts to life through the art of storytelling. One of the best-loved stories about death is the story of an encounter between the Buddha and a woman who had lost her only son. The woman was deeply distraught and came to the Buddha, convinced that he had supernatural power and could bring her son back to life. The Buddha agreed to do what she asked, if she could bring him a seed from a household in her village that had not suffered a similar loss. She went from house to house, heard one story after another of family members who had died, and came back to the Buddha to tell him that all had suffered losses similar to hers. She said something else as well: she realized in her sad journey from house to house that death was part of life and even her grievous loss was something that could be accepted and allowed to pass away.

This attitude of wise acceptance has been a crucial part of the Buddhist approach to death from ancient times and has colored not just the way Buddhists look at the final moments of their lives but at the flow of life itself. I once made the mistake (fairly common among beginning students of Buddhism) of asking a Buddhist monk, who was said to be the reincarnation of an important Tibetan lama, whether he could tell me about his previous lives. He laughed and said that he could hardly remember what he had eaten for breakfast, let alone what he had experienced in a previous life. I took his comment to be more than a graceful exit from an embarrassing question. It typified for me a deep-seated Buddhist respect for the flow and changeableness of life. Buddhists sometimes say that it is no more difficult to believe that the same person can die and be reborn in another body than to believe that I can wake up in the morning and think that I am the same person who went to sleep the night before. The process of life—the evolution of each personality—is a process of constant change. What I was yesterday is gone. What I am now is just a flickering moment in the process of becoming something new. Life itself is a process of death and rebirth. And a wise, attentive attitude toward life involves a graceful acceptance of the death in the midst of each passing moment that allows everything to become new.

THE TIBETAN BOOK OF THE DEAD

One of the most striking examples of a Buddhist response to death that is also a meditation for the living is the text known as the *Tibetan Book of the Dead*.[8] This text, used by Buddhists in Tibet and the border areas of the Himalayas as a ritual guidebook, is recited to a person who has recently died in order to help the dead person's consciousness navigate through the experiences of the afterlife. The text depicts the intermediate state (*Bar-do*) between one life and the next as a three-stage process. Each stage presents the consciousness of the dead person with a new set of challenges and opportunities. At each stage the consciousness runs the risk of being bewildered and falling back into a painful birth in this world, but it also has the opportunity of hearing and attending to the teaching of the text in such a way that it can avoid being reborn. (For this reason, the text is known in Tibetan as the *Bar-do Thos-grol*, or "Liberation through Hearing in the Intermediate State.") Even if consciousness fails to escape the process of rebirth completely, it can use the teaching of the text to control the location of its next birth and give itself a better opportunity for liberation in the next life.

In the first stage, known as the '*Chi-ka'i Bar-do* (the *Bar-do* of the moment of death), the consciousness of the dead person merges into a state of pure, nondualistic awareness. Consciousness is aware of no object apart from itself and glows in the fullness of its own luminosity. The text says that its instructions about this stage should begin, if possible, even before the actual moment of death:

> O son of noble family, (name), listen. . . . This mind of yours is inseparable luminosity and emptiness in the form of a great mass of light, it has no birth or death, therefore it is the buddha of Immortal Light. To recognize this is all that is necessary. When you recognize this pure nature of your mind as the buddha, looking into your own mind is resting in the buddha-mind.[9]

This instruction about the nature of the mind is supposed to be spoken to the dying person by name and should be repeated several times in a clear voice. If the consciousness of the dying person recognizes this state of luminous awareness as its own nature, it merges into it and is freed from rebirth.

In the next stage of the text (known as the *Chos-nyid Bar-do*, the intermediate state that is identified with the nature of reality), the consciousness of the dead person confronts the projection of its own fears and desires in a series of Buddha-images. These Buddha-images appear first in peaceful form and then in a form that is angry and threatening. The forms are similar to the *thangka* paintings Tibetans use as guides for meditation, and are painted on small cards to be shown to the consciousness of the dead person while the descriptions of the images are being recited from text itself. At each step in the process, the recitation of the text is meant to calm the consciousness of the dead person and teach it to recognize the images as projections of itself. If consciousness is able to recognize the images as its own manifestations, it can merge with them and escape the cycle of rebirth.

The first images are of peaceful Buddhas, but even these peaceful images terrify the unsuspecting mind with their brightness and intensity. The text warns that each image will be accompanied by a great roar of thunder, like a thousand thunderclaps sounding simultaneously, and it says that the dead person's consciousness should remember that it has lost its physical body and the images will do it no harm. The first image in this sequence is of the Buddha Vairocana (the Buddha associated with the sun). His body is white, he sits on a lion throne, he holds an eight-spoked wheel in his hand, and he embraces his female counterpart, the Queen of the Realm of Space. From the heart of Vairocana comes a blue light, representing consciousness itself. The light is so intense that consciousness can hardly bear it. At the same time, consciousness becomes aware of a softer and more inviting light that comes from the realm of the gods. The text explains that consciousness will be distracted by the residues of its previous actions and try to escape from the intense light of Vairocana. At the same time, it will be attracted by the soft light of the gods. This attraction must be resisted if consciousness wants to escape rebirth.

> Do not take pleasure in the soft white light of the gods, do not be attracted to it or yearn for it. If you are attracted to it you will wander into the realm of the gods and circle among the six kinds of existence. It is an obstacle blocking the path of liberation, so do not look at it, but feel longing for the bright blue light, and repeat this inspiration-prayer after me with intense concentration on Blessed Vairocana: "When through intense ignorance I

wander in saṃsāra, on the luminous light-path of the dharma-
dhātu wisdom, may Blessed Vairocana go before me, his consort
the Queen of Vajra Space behind me; help me to cross the bardo's
dangerous pathway and bring me to the perfect buddha state." By
saying this inspiration-prayer with deep devotion, he will dissolve
into the rainbow light in the heart of Vairocana and his consort.[10]

If consciousness lets opportunities like this slip by, it enters the
Srid-pa'i Bar-do, the state of "becoming." Here consciousness slowly
turns from the challenge of escaping the cycle to the challenge of controlling and manipulating the place where it will be reborn. Escape is
still a possibility if consciousness can fix itself in a state of pure awareness and not be tossed around by the winds of fear and desire, but the
storms become even more intense, and the lure of reentry into the
world becomes even more difficult to resist. If consciousness fails to
follow any of the directions of the text, it may end up with a vision of a
dung heap, be wrapped up in the sweetness of its smell, and be reborn
as a worm.

To grasp the full significance of the *Tibetan Book of the Dead*, it
is important to recognize that there is more to its audience than just
the dead person's consciousness. The text also belongs to the living, to
the religious specialists who recite it and to friends and relatives who
listen to its recitation—to all those, in other words, who use it to ease the
dead person's passage into the next life and, in the process, ease their
own thoughts and fears about death. The days of mourning and the
solemn rituals that accompany them give the dead person's friends and
family a chance to express their grief and heal the wound that death
creates in their community and their world. It is no accident that the
recitation of the text ends with the burning of the picture that represents the personality of the deceased. At the end even the image of the
dead person has to be renounced so that he or she can move beyond
this world and the mourners can return to their own lives.

But the connection between the ritual for the dead and the lives
of the living is even more direct than this. The text does not just map
the stages of the afterlife; it charts the evolution of consciousness itself,
for the living as well as for the dead. The friends, family, and ritual specialists who sit through the ceremony come face to face with their own
images of the terrifying brightness of consciousness, the shadowy images of wrath and destruction that lurk beneath the surface of the mind,

and the alluring images of life in the world of rebirth. They have an opportunity to contemplate their fears and let them go as they learn to relax their grip on the consciousness of the person who has died. When they do this, they also come face to face with an aspect of Buddhist teaching that goes back, it seems, to the Buddha himself. For Buddhists, death is an inescapable and essential part of life, not just at the moment when the body ceases to function and consciousness begins its journey into the afterlife, but in the flow of life itself. To allow each moment to "die" and make itself new is to experience some of the stillness and luminosity that the *Tibetan Book of the Dead* teaches to the living as well as the dead.

THE PURE LAND TRADITION

While it may be one of the most elaborate, the ritual associated with the *Tibetan Book of the Dead* is by no means the only way Buddhists have attempted to contemplate and guide the process of death and rebirth. Chinese and Japanese Buddhists have developed a rich tradition of meditation on the figure of Amitābha Buddha (called Amida Buddha in Japan) at the moment of death. According to this tradition, any person who hears the name of the Buddha Amitābha ("Infinite Light") or Amitāyuḥ ("Infinite Life") and meditates on it at the moment of death will be visited by Amitābha and carried away to a heavenly realm. The Indian tradition refers to this realm as "the Pleasurable" (*Sukhāvatī*). It is known more commonly as the Pure Land. The Pure Land tradition stems from a group of Indian Buddhist texts about the process that led to Amitābha Buddha's awakening. Before his awakening, Amitābha (or, more accurately, the bodhisattva who was to become Amitābha at the moment of his awakening) made the following vow:

> If those beings who have directed their thoughts toward the highest perfect knowledge in other worlds, and who, after having heard my name, when I have reached awakening, have meditated on me with serene thoughts; if at the moment of their death, after having approached them, surrounded by an assembly of monks, I should not stand before them, worshipped by them, so their thoughts may not be troubled, then may I not obtain the highest perfect knowledge.

This Buddhist practice of invoking a deity at the moment of death was widespread in India in the first few centuries of the Common Era. The *Bhagavad Gītā* attributes a similar promise to Krishna, in a passage where Krishna says that all who remember him at the moment of death will come to him.[11] Both the Hindu and Buddhist traditions use the word "remember" (*smṛti* or *anusmṛti*) to refer to a variety of meditative practices (not unlike the Christian concept of "recollection"). *Smṛti* can be understood simply as "mindfulness." As *anusmṛti*, it has the more active or constructive function of "visualization." Unlike the meditations that seek to calm the mind and empty it of all images, the act of visualization is meant to fill the mind with an intense image of the heavenly being that the believer hopes to be united with after death. And it was not necessary in the Indian tradition even to wait for the moment of death. There are accounts of Buddhist monks and devotees who fasted and prayed in the hope of being given a vision of the heavenly world in this life. We even read of travelers who fell into the hands of pirates and robbers and managed to escape from danger by visualizing a journey into the heavenly world.[12]

One of the most important components in Pure Land Buddhism as it is practiced today in Japan and America (notably by the Buddhist Churches of America) is the chanting of Amitābha Buddha's name. This practice is called the *nembutsu* and consists of repeating the phrase *Namu Amida Butsu* ("Homage to Amitābha Buddha"). The scriptural accounts of Amitābha's vows stress the need to hear Amitābha's name and chant it with faith. So the "remembrance" of the Buddha that lies at the heart of Pure Land Buddhism does not need to be thought of as "visualization" in an elaborate or technical sense. It can simply be the act of calling on the Buddha's name with a pure heart. With this act a person invokes the power of Amitābha's compassion and connects to the promise of the Pure Land.

While the recitation of the *nembutsu* grows out of the ancient Indian practice of meditation at the moment of death, it also, like the *Tibetan Book of the Dead*, has a strong connection with meditation that focuses the mind in moments of danger or discouragement in the middle of this life. The shift of focus from the moment of death to the process of life has deep roots in Japanese tradition and carries with it a shift in the understanding of the Pure Land itself. The priest Ryoyo in 1385 said that the ordinary conception of the soul's being transported to Paradise and born there was merely a figure of speech. . . , the fact being that neither Amida, nor the sainted beings, nor the "nine ranks" are to be conceived as existing "over there" at all, because the Pure Land is the ultimate and absolute reality, and that is everywhere, so that we may be identified with it right here where we are.

ZEN POEMS AT THE MOMENT OF DEATH

Another Buddhist tradition associated with the moment of death is the Japanese Zen practice of composing a verse to express the condition of the mind at the moment when one is taking leave from this world. Some of the poems grew out of the violent lives of the samurai, where death could come swiftly and a warrior could be compelled by his sense of honor to die at his own hand. One such poem, written as a warrior was to commit ritual suicide, speaks eloquently of the Buddhist ideal of stillness in the midst of suffering.

> The sharp-edged sword, unsheathed,
> Cuts through the void—
> Within the raging fire
> A cool wind blows.[13]

Here the sword that brings the warrior's death represents the sword of wisdom that cuts through the illusions of this world. The image of life as a raging fire is an ancient Buddhist image of suffering. In the end, the only way to extinguish this fire is with the wisdom of the Buddha. Other poems speak of the world as a dream and of death as a moment of awakening.

> Throughout the frosty night
> I lay awake. When morning bells
> rang out, my heart grew clear—
> upon this fleeting dream-world
> dawn is waking.[14]

The movement of thought in both these poems is the reverse of the movement that characterized the *Tibetan Book of the Dead* and the texts of the Pure Land. There the focus on death and the meditations that accompanied it came first and were then appropriated as guides for the living. Here we see a lifetime of detachment and concentration distilled into a few short lines at the moment of death. It is not surprising that there was a movement within the Japanese tradition of death poems to reverse the process and see all of a person's life (and all of a person's poetry) as expressing an awareness of death. When the great poet Bashō (1644–94) lay on his deathbed and his pupils hinted that he ought to leave them a death poem, he said that any of his poems could be considered a meditation on death.

Bashō was a great traveler and had a remarkable ability to capture the experience of sadness when he took leave from a place that he loved, as in the poem that starts his famous *Narrow Road to the Deep North.*

> Behind this door
> Now buried in deep grass,
> A different generation will celebrate
> The Festival of the Dolls.[15]

The remnants of a long-dead warrior's armor could elicit in Bashō the same sense of melancholy:

> I am awe-struck
> To hear a cricket singing
> Underneath the dark cavity
> Of an old helmet.[16]

Bashō's poetry shares a deep kinship with the *Tibetan Book of the Dead* and the tradition of Pure Land Buddhism, and all three shared this kinship with the story of Siddhārtha Gautama himself. All were concerned with death. In one way or another, each of them taught people to face death squarely, to be freed from its terrors, and to accept its presence as part of life. They refused to separate themselves from the experience of death or treat death as something that lay only at the end of life. I said earlier that Buddhists insist that a wise attitude toward life involves a graceful acceptance of death in the midst of each passing moment. I also said that one of the most important things Buddhists do is prepare for death. That is true, but it is only part of the truth. It is just as true to say that Buddhists prepare to live, and their meditation on death is a crucial part of their preparation to be fully alive.

DEATH AND AWAKENING AMONG THE PHILOSOPHERS

It is easy to understand that Buddhists might find it easier to live happy lives if they are not constantly afraid of death. But this simple observation leaves a number of important questions unanswered. We know that death lies at the end of life, but what does it mean to say that there is death in the midst of life? And what does an awareness of death have to do with "awakening"? For that matter, what does it mean for Buddhists to say that they are "fully alive"? Do these words have any clear meaning, or are they religious metaphors, useful to comfort those who grieve or to motivate those who have lost their taste for life but incorrigibly vague when it comes to the hard, analytical task of connecting words with things?

Modern Buddhists often insist that Buddhism is not just a theory: it has to be realized in practice. The distinction between "theory" and "practice" is as misleading in Buddhist sources, however, as it is in the classical sources of the Western tradition. For Aristotle *theoria* ("contemplation" or simply "vision") was an eminently "practical" virtue, at least in the modern sense of the word "practice."[17] *Theoria* made it possible for people to "get the picture," to see things as they are and, with a changed perception of the nature of things, to live a more complete, more satisfying, or more virtuous life. Buddhist philosophers made the same connection between vision and life. The Buddha's first sermon, a text that functioned as a blueprint for the development of Buddhist philosophy, pictured the Buddha's awakening as an act of vision. The Buddha told his first group of disciples that his practice of the path had led him to vision, knowledge, calm, insight, and nirvana.[18] Here the word "vision" (*darśana*) implied that the Buddha no longer had to accept someone else's account of the truth: he could see it for himself. The concept of vision recurred in the language of the philosophers. Philosophical systems were called "visions" (*darśana*) of "reality" (*tattva*), and the pursuit of reality was closely related to the discipline we call "meditation." Buddhist practitioners disciplined the mind in two ways: by "calming" (*śamatha*) its fluctuations and by "discerning" (*vipaśyanā*) the nature of reality. The word "discernment" (*vipaśyanā*, which is often translated "insight") means literally to "see apart." Buddhist philosophers made it clear that their philosophy began with the attempt to distinguish one thing from another or, more accurately, to distinguish reality from illusion. The act of distinction was a form of vision.

Hans Jonas said that "sight has been hailed as the most excellent of the senses" since the days of the Greeks.[19] Much of what he said about the language of vision in Western philosophy can be applied directly to Buddhism. Vision allows someone to take in a whole scene simultaneously rather than to process it as a sequence of sensations through the medium of sound or touch. It also makes it possible to neutralize sensory involvement with the object. Unlike the sense of hearing, sight can by turned off simply by shutting the eyes. Finally, the possibility of seeing from a distance, perhaps even a very great distance, makes vision the model for concepts of infinity. To these three characteristics (all mentioned by Jonas), Buddhist philosophers added a fourth. Unlike the sense of hearing, sight gives direct access to things. Rather than having to take someone else's word for things, sight makes it possible to see for oneself. This feature of the visual sense was so fundamental to a Buddhist understanding of perception that the Buddha's own teaching was called the *ehipassika dhamma*, the "come and see" teaching.

The metaphor of knowing as seeing suggested that a person would be better off on a mountain, where the whole landscape could be surveyed in a single act of vision, rather than in the valley. The metaphor of knowing as going also had spatial implications. To know something correctly, it was better to follow the correct "path" (*pratipad* or *mārga*) than to wander to one side or the other. The correct path, in other words, was one that avoided extremes, as the Buddha said in the opening lines of his first sermon:

> Bhikkhus, these two extremes ought not to be practised by one who has set forth from the household life. What are the two? There is devotion to the indulgence of sense-pleasures, which is low, common, the way of ordinary people, unworthy, and unprofitable; and there is devotion to self-mortification, which is painful, unworthy, and unprofitable. Avoiding both these extremes, the Tathāgata has realised the Middle Path: it gives vision, it give knowledge, and it leads to calm, to insight, to enlightenment, to Nibbāna.

Howard Nemerov has said that metaphors often function as compressed stories.[20] It is not hard to imagine how the two basic metaphors of Buddhist philosophy—knowing as seeing and knowing as going— can be spun out into an infinite number of complex stories.

The metaphorical framework of Buddhist philosophy gave these stories a certain predictable shape. When Buddhists probed the reference of problematic words like "death" and "awakening," they posed their questions in certain ways. Correct solutions were ones that favored direct, unmediated understanding over understanding that came through words, concepts, or images. The analytical process itself moved through a series of negations, as if the philosopher were climbing a mountain and leaving a series of partial or misleading perceptions behind: false concepts were abandoned until nothing but the correct awareness remained. But the goal could not be nothingness, pure and simple. Philosophical reasoning had to follow a "middle path" between extremes. It could not affirm too much without becoming a source of attachment; it could not deny too much without becoming harsh and unproductive. The key to interpreting a Buddhist philosophical system is to find the subtle ways each thinker tries to follow the path to the top of the mountain without straying into one of the unworthy and unprofitable extremes.

A good example of the way Buddhist philosophers pick their way along the trail of Buddhist thought comes from a late, semi-canonical Pali text (ca. 200 C.E.) called *The Questions of King Milinda*.[21] The text reports a series of conversations between the Buddhist monk Nāgasena and a Greek king by the name of Menander (Milinda in Pali) in one of the Greek kingdoms left behind in Gandhara by the invasion of Alexander the Great. In one of the conversations, the king asks Nāgasena about the Buddhist concept of "no-self." According to basic Buddhist doctrine, everything is impermanent, and because everything is impermanent, nothing has any enduring identity or "self" (*ātman*). The king asks Nāgasena what the name "Nāgasena" refers to if there is no continuous self. Nāgasena answers with a question: How did the king come to the meeting, on foot or in a chariot? The king says that a man of his station would only come in a chariot. Nāgasena then asks what the word "chariot" refers to. Does it designate the pole, the wheels, the boards, or something constituent of the so-called "chariot"? The king replies that it does not actually refer to any of these things. It is a simply a conventional designation that depends on these individual parts. Nāgasena then uses the king's own words to explain the meaning of the word "Nāgasena." He says that it does not actually refer to anything: it is only a conventional designation that depends on a series of momentary constituents. Here it is not enough just to negate the "self." The negative claim has to be balanced with a positive claim. Otherwise Nāga-sena's position would fall into an extreme. So he says that, although there is no self, it is still possible to use the word "self" in a conventional way, with reference to or depending on the momentary constituents of the personality.

This little philosophical tale gives a good picture of the constraints that limit Buddhist answers to questions about "death" and "awakening." To say that there is death in the midst of each passing moment means that everything is impermanent: each moment in the flow of existence ceases, and its cessation is followed by something new. It also means that the words people use to refer to seemingly stable things are actually illusory: they do not name anything real. At most, they are conventional designations, useful for negotiating the practical details of life, but incapable of naming something that is ultimately real. In this picture of the world, the word "death" refers first to the "cessation" (*nirodha*) of each individual moment as it gives way to something new. But in the life of a Buddha, the cessation of each individual moment leads to a more definitive cessation. Buddhists call this final cessation nirvana, the "blowing out" of the fire of suffering, ignorance, and desire. From a subjective point of view the "death" of each individual moment in the flow of reality mirrors a "death" in the mind of the practitioner. Illusions stop, and with the illusions go all the emotional ties that connect a person to the world of death and rebirth. The chief of these illusions, of course, is the illusion of a permanent "self."

Understood this way, "death" comes very close to what Buddhists mean by "awakening" (*bodhi*). The normal English translation of the word *bodhi* is "enlightenment." Why we translate it this way has never, to my knowledge, been adequately explained. Buddhist commentaries make it clear that the word *bodhi* has two possible interpretations. It can mean that the Buddha has "awakened" (*prabuddha*) from the dream of ignorance, or it can mean that the Buddha's intelligence has "blossomed" (*vibuddha*) like a lotus. The earliest Tibetan translators created an artificial, bisyllabic code word *saṅs-rgyas* ("awake-expand") to squeeze these two meanings into Tibetan. In English we are normally content just to replace "enlightenment" with the more accurate "awakening," perhaps because it does not seem to convey the requisite *gravitas* to say in English that the Buddha has "blossomed." In any case, the word "awakening" adds a third metaphor for knowledge. The practice of philosophy is intended, philosophers say, to peel away the layers of illusion as if one were dispelling the illusions of a dream. When the metaphor of awakening is elaborated, it often converges with the metaphor of vision, although in a negative mode. If you want to see the phantoms of a dream as they really are, the best way is not to see them at all. The experience of awakening is sometimes compared to the experience of looking at the sky from the top of a mountain on an autumn day: no clouds, nothing to see, no vision, awakening.

Mahāyāna philosophers, of whom the first and perhaps most famous was Nāgārjuna (ca. second century c.e.), formulated the doctrine of "no self" in a radical way. They argued that it was not only impossible to seek and grasp any permanent or enduring reality in things; it was also impossible to find any momentary constituents in things. In other words, nothing existed in its own right even for a moment. The customary way of expressing this point was to say that all of the possible categories of reality are empty (śūnya) of identity (svabhāva), including, of course, emptiness itself. This approach lent itself naturally to paradox. The basic sources of the Mahāyāna tradition were fond of statements like: "Form is emptiness and emptiness is form" and "The bodhisattva should vow to lead all beings to awakening, and the bodhisattva should understand that there are no beings to be led to awakening, and there is no awakening." But it also flirted dangerously with the constraints of the Middle Path. If these early Mahāyāna philosophers thought that nothing is real, how could they avoid a conceptual version of the old extreme of self-mortification? If everything is empty, even the momentary constituents of the "self," how could anyone take seriously the moral or intellectual demands of the Buddhist path?

The early philosophers of the Mahāyāna, especially those who carried on the tradition of Nāgārjuna, argued that everything was empty ultimately but still functioned according to the logic and expectations of conventional reality—the logic, you might say, of a dream. They even turned the criticism of the Mahāyāna around and said that emptiness did not deny possibilities; it was the condition of all possibilities. "Everything is possible," Nāgārjuna says, "for someone for whom emptiness is possible; nothing is possible for someone for whom emptiness is not possible."[22] Here Nāgārjuna specifies in an even more radical way what it means for a Buddhist to cultivate "a graceful acceptance of the death that comes in the midst of each passing moment and allows each moment to become new." "Death" is the cessation of any concept of identity, not just between moments but in the moments themselves. For Mahāyāna philosophers this is the cessation that constitutes the Buddha's awakening.

THE BUDDHIST USE OF THE WORD "JUST"

When Buddhists talk about emptiness, it is important to listen for a subtle change in inflection when the concept of emptiness has been carried to its logical conclusion and conversation turns again to the conventional details of life. A few years ago, the Dalai Lama gave a lecture at Harvard on the no-self doctrine. At the end of a long discourse in Tibetan about the reasons nothing has any identity, he paused and asked: "If there is no self, who just told you this?" His answer in Tibetan was *bdag tsam*. In English we would say, "the mere I" or "just me." The word "mere" or "just" (Sanskrit *mātra* or Tibetan *tsam*) developed the status of a technical term in late Indian Mahāyāna thought. Philosophers came to use it as a way of referring to conventional reality after all illusions about its ultimate identity have been removed.[23] The most intriguing aspect of the word, however, lies not in its technical weight but in its lightness. The Dalai Lama used the word in a playful way, with a hint of a smile, as if the logic of emptiness did not lead to blankness and futility, but to a sense of lightness and freedom.

The reason for the Dalai Lama's shift in tone is not difficult to find in the works of the Indian philosophers, although it helps to know where to look. The arguments about emptiness in the tradition that stemmed from Nāgārjuna were often organized in three separate stages. The first stage began with conventional categories and assumed the distinctions of conventional truth. In the second stage, these categories were "analyzed" (*vicaryate*) to find the reference of conventional words. The result of this stage, of course, was emptiness, the absence of real identity. This might seem to be the conclusion of the argument—the peak of the mountain, as it were, with the most definitive vision of the empty space beyond. But the most important move in this system of thought came in the next stage, when the analytical approach of the second stage was applied to the concept of emptiness itself. In the end, when emptiness and conventional truth were analyzed from the ultimate point of view, there was no real distinction between them.

This logical move led the philosophers back to a reappropriation of the distinctions of conventional truth, viewed from the perspective of emptiness.

In the work of the philosophers, the third stage of thought had a number of unusual logical features. It involved, for example, a distinctive use of the metaphor of knowledge as "finding" or "grasping." When things were analyzed from the ultimate point of view, there was nothing to "find" or "grasp." Correct knowledge of a thing involved "no grasping" (*anupalabdhi*): to grasp it correctly was not to grasp it at all. But the most intriguing feature had to do with the sense of lightness and freedom in the Dalai Lama's use of the word "just." If there was nothing to grasp, there was nothing to be grasped by and nothing to fear. "Self" could be used with the hint of a smile and with a sense of playful detachment.

Bashō's strength as a Buddhist poet depended not just on his ability to capture the tone of sadness in the passing of each moment but also on a quality known to Japanese critics as *okashi*, "a kind of irreverence or humorous detachment [a "no-grasping" attitude] toward the absurdity of life."[24] His most famous poem is a three-line *haiku*:

> Old pond,
> Frog jumps in,
> Sound of water.[25]

It is sometimes said that the whole meaning of Buddhism is summed up in these lines.[26] Certainly the poem distills the intellectual movement of the three levels of truth. The old pond is a symbol of emptiness: it is quiet, unaffected by the flow of time. Into this stillness comes a conventional event: the jump of a frog. In the third line, emptiness and conventional truth merge in the perception of a single sound. In the Zen tradition it is an experience of awakening to be fully present to a single moment of perception.

The poem does not come fully to life, however, until it is read as a commentary, not just on the three levels of truth, but on the relationship between the poet's words and the mind of the reader. If the old pond is the reader's mind, the frog must be the poet, and the poem must be the sound of water, a fusion of the poet and the reader in a moment of perception. The irreverent playfulness in this reading lies in the equation of the poet and the frog. It is not entirely bad in Japanese tradition to suggest that there is a kinship between humans and animals, even between humans and frogs. For a Zen master to sit or move naturally is a great achievement; if a poet could actually speak naturally, the way a frog leaps, it would be a form of awakening. But human beings also are human precisely in the way they distinguish themselves from animals, especially in the exquisitely refined cultural creation of a Japanese poem.[27] By playing across the gap between nature and culture, and between poet and reader, the poem puts into play some of the most fundamental ambiguities in Japanese Buddhism and in Japanese culture as a whole. The fact that these ambiguities are irresolvable just makes them that much more lively and amusing.

One of the questions that provoked this excursion into the world of the philosophers had to do with the problematic and elusive phenomenon we call, for lack of a better word, life: What would it mean for Buddhists to say that they feel "fully alive"? The truth is that it is no easier to answer this question in Buddhist terms than it is in terms of other religious traditions. But the sense of playfulness in the concept of emptiness suggests a possible Buddhist answer. The pursuit of emptiness is intensely serious and intensely negative: it is meant to free the mind from all forms of attachment and illusion. But, in the end, it leads back to the conventional world with a sense of lightness and freedom. This is why the concept of emptiness is amusing and full of life. In the end, this also may be the most important point of connection not only with the child's verses of *The New England Primer* but with the religious milieu out of which they come.

The *Primer's* verses raised one of the most serious religious problems for the Puritan imagination: how to ask God to keep my soul at the moment of death when the fate of my soul and every other soul has already been determined. Simply to ask the question casts the heart and mind into a bottomless paradox. Yet how could the question not be asked? And if the unaskable question must be asked, if the question fractures logic and stops thought, what better way to ask it than in the sing-song rhythms of a child?[28] The prayer does not solve the question; it simply puts the question into play by playing across the Christian paradox of freedom the way Bashō played across the Buddhist paradox of emptiness. "To contemplate the perils of death, seek awakening, and do it all with the playful spirit of a child" might even be a good definition of religion.[29] Certainly it is one in which Buddhists would feel very much at home.

NOTES

1. John Bartlett, *Familiar Quotations: A collection of passages, phrases, and proverbs traced to their sources in ancient and modern literature*, 15th ed., ed. Emily Morison Beck (Boston: Little, Brown & Co., 1982), p. 320.

2. Paul Leicester Ford, ed., *The New England Primer: A History of Its Origin and Development* (New York: Columbia University, 1962). The ascription of this poem to John Rogers is considered apocryphal.

3. David E. Stannard has explored this question with remarkable sensitivity in *The Puritan Way of Death: A Study in Religion, Culture, and Social Change* (New York: Oxford University Press, 1977).

4. The prayer read as follows in the *Primer* of 1784:

> Now I lay me down to sleep,
> I pray the Lord my soul to keep;
> If I should die before I wake,
> I pray the Lord my soul to take.

5. Dharmasena Thera, *Jewels of the Doctrine: Stories of the Saddharma Ratnāvaliya*, trans. Ranjini Obeyesekere (Albany: State University of New York Press, 1991), p. x.

6. E. B. Cowell, ed., *The Jātaka or Stories of the Buddha's Former Births* (Cambridge: Cambridge University Press, 1895; reprint ed., Delhi: Motilal Banarsidass, 1994).

7. *Mahavastu* 1.359–66; *Jātaka* 12.

8. W. Y. Evans-Wentz, *The Tibetan Book of the Dead* (London: Oxford University Press, 1927; third ed.,1957); Francesca Fremantle and Chogyam Trungpa, *The Tibetan Book of the Dead: The Great Liberation Through Hearing in the Bardo* (Boulder, Colo.: Shambhala, 1975).

9. Fremantle and Trungpa, *Tibetan Book of the Dead*, p. 37.

10. Ibid., p. 42.

11. *Bhagavad Gītā* 8.4: "Anyone who remembers me at the moment of death, leaves the body, and goes forth, goes to me; of this there is no doubt" (*antakāle ca mām eva smaran muktvā kalevaram / yaḥ prayāti sa madbhāvam yāti nāsty atra saṃśayaḥ*). This verse echoes the last verse of the seventh chapter: "Those who know me as the inner being, inner deity, and inner sacrifice have disciplined their minds and know me at the time of death (lit. at the time of their going forth)."

12. I discuss the active function of *anusmṛti* in chapter 7 of my book *To See the Buddha: A Philosopher's Quest for the Meaning of Emptiness* (Princeton: Princeton University Press, 1994).

13. Yoel Hoffmann, *Japanese Death Poems Written by Zen Monks and Haiku Poets on the Verge of Death* (Rutland, Vt.: Charles E. Tuttle, 1986), p. 51.

14. Ibid., p. 67.

15. Matsuo Bashō, *The Narrow Road to the Deep North and Other Travel Sketches* (Harmondsworth, Middlesex: Penguin, 1966), p. 98. The experience I call "melancholy" (*mono-no-aware*) has had the status of a technical concept in the Japanese literary criticism since Motoori Norinaga (1730–1801) identified it as the sentiment of literature in the Heian Period (794–1185). *Mono-no-aware* involves a compassionate understanding of the impermanence of life. In Mahāyāna Buddhism, compassion and understanding (especially understanding of the impermanence of things) are the two principal components of a Buddha's enlightenment.

The translator in the Penguin edition of Bashō has expanded the three lines of Bashō's *haiku* to four to unpack some of his cryptic cultural references. Cid Corman and Kamaike Susumu give a more literal translation in *Back Roads to Far Towns: Basho's Travel Journal* (Fredonia, N.Y.: White Pine Press, 1986): "the grass door also / turning and turning into / a doll's household."

16. Bashō, *Narrow Road*, p. 134.

17. According to Alexander Nehamas, "Even when Aristotle identified philosophy with 'theory,' his purpose was to argue, as he does in the tenth and last book of the *Nicomachean Ethics*, that a *life* of theoretical activity, the life of philosophy, was the best life that human beings could live" (Nehamas, *The Art of Living: Socratic Reflections from Plato to Foucault* (Berkeley: University of California Press, 1998), p. 2. Pierre Hadot makes a similar argument in *Philosophy as a Way of Life*, trans. Michael Chase (Oxford: Blackwell, 1995).

18. "Avoiding both extremes, the Tathāgata has realized the Middle Path: it gives vision, it gives knowledge, and it leads to calm, to insight, to enlightenment, to Nibbāna." "The Discourse on Turning the Wheel of the Dharma" (*Dhammacakkappavattana Sutta*) is widely translated in collections of Buddhist scriptures. This translation is quoted from Walpola Rahula, *What the Buddha Taught* (New York: Grove Press, 1974).

19. Hans Jonas, "The Nobility of Sight: A Study in the Phenomenology of the Senses," in *The Phenomenon of Life: Toward a Philosophical Biology* (New York: Harper & Row, 1966), pp. 135–56.

20. Howard Nemerov, "On Metaphor," in *A Howard Nemerov Reader* (Columbia, Mo.: University of Missouri Press, 1991), pp. 223–36.

21. T. W. Rhys Davids, trans., *The Questions of King Milinda*, Sacred Books of the East, vols. 35–36 (Oxford: Clarendon Press, 1890–94; reprint ed. New York: Dover Publications, 1963).

22. Nāgārjuna, *Mūlamadhyamakakārikāḥ*, ed. J. W. de Jong (Madras: Adyar Library and Research Centre, 1977), 24.14.

23. For a good example in the eighth-century followers of Nāgārjuna, see Malcolm David Eckel, *Jñanagarbha's Commentary on the Distinction Between the Two Truths* (Albany: State University of New York Press, 1987).

24. Makoto Ooka, as quoted by William H. Honan, in "Why Millions in Japan Read All About Poetry," *New York Times*, 6 March 2000.

25. This verse has been widely translated, as Hiroaki Sato amply demonstrated in *One Hundred Frogs: From Renga to Haiku in English* (New York: Weatherhill, 1983). The translation quoted here is a distillation of several of the most commonly quoted English versions.

26. Robert S. Ellwood and Richard Pilgrim, *Japanese Religion* (Englewood Cliffs, N.J.: Prentice-Hall, 1985), p. 55.

27. Emiko Ohnuki-Tierney has commented on the ambiguities in Japanese attitudes toward the relationship of humans and animals in "Embedding and Transforming Polytrope: The Monkey as Self in Japanese Culture," in *Beyond Metaphor: The Theory of Tropes in Anthropology*, ed. James W. Fernandez (Stanford, Calif.: Stanford University Press, 1991), pp. 159–89. On the relationship of "nature" and "culture" in the Buddhist tradition more generally, see Malcolm David Eckel, "Is There a Buddhist Philosophy of Nature?" in *Philosophies of Nature: The Human Dimension*, ed. Robert S. Cohen and Alfred I. Tauber (Dordrecht: Kluwer Academic Publishers, 1998), pp. 53–69.

28. It is the childlike naiveté of the language in Ernest Hemingway's short story "Now I Lay Me" that gives his treatment of this prayer such uncanny power (Hemingway, *The Short Stories* [New York: Scribner, 1997], pp. 332–39).

29. The element of incongruity and playfulness in different aspects of religious expression has been an important theme in the theoretical work of Jonathan Z. Smith, as it has been in the work of others before him. For commentary on this aspect of Smith's work, see Sam Gill, "No Place to Stand: Jonathan Z. Smith as *Homo Ludens*, The Academic Study of Religion *Sub Specie Ludi*," *Journal of the American Academy of Religion* 66 (1998): 283–312.

A Rose for the Buddha:
In Response to David Eckel

BRIAN W. JORGENSEN

SURELY ONE OF the things that is going to be notable about our times is the deepening and expanding dialogue between East and West, which David Eckel has carried forward on a number of different levels, not least the meeting of the *New England Primer* and the Tibetan *Book of the Dead*. What strikes me about that wonderful meeting is the stern quaintness of the one and the moving, luminous, post-humane quality of the other. I say "post-humane" because the *Book of the Dead* denies the ultimate reality of what we ordinarily mean by human, yet could not properly be characterized as inhuman, or inhumane. Indeed, the *New England Primer* has the starker reliance on a transcendence which is only to be found past the borders, firmly drawn and abysmally deep, of the human. In addition, whereas the *New England Primer* suggests that the divine and otherworldly sternness is what we first need to learn from, the *Book of the Dead* teaches that the inhuman is properly reached through the humane. The *Book of the Dead's* orientation is toward release and assuagement, that is, human longings; toward compassion, a human attitude toward the human condition; in a word, toward what David Eckel has taught me the Buddhists call mercy. These human promptings are to be taken, the *Book of the Dead* teaches, as vehicles pointing toward a knowledge which is at the very heart of being human—but that knowledge, its subject and object, is not human. Ultimately, in the name of mercy, the human essence must be, not corrected and refined, as in the primer, but discouraged and dissolved as the illusion it is. Reading the *Book of the Dead* seems to me, then, an odd experience for which an odd word might be needed. Reading with an attempt at realization, the still-human mind finds itself, in the name of mercy toward the human, in the post-humane place. There is a strangeness and coolness about that place. There is a

94

perpetual feeling of goodbye and even, for the mind trained by, say, Aristotle, a sense of betrayal of the *politikon zoon*, the political animal humans are said to be. The human mind wonders uneasily if the coolness of the post-humane place could shade into a coldness, especially if the memory of the humane intention, the humane path to the place, were to fade.

Certainly there are souls today—and I grant that, in this context, the word "soul" sounds inappropriate; perhaps I may be allowed to use it just as a temporary way of speaking—there are souls that seem to prefer what I am calling the post-humane, to feel that this is what they have been seeking. One might guess that they are the reincarnations of those for whom Stoicism, including its account of the cosmos, was the truest guide. But I wonder if the feelings of these souls—feelings that resonate with thought—may not be generalized to something less individual, more in our air at this historical moment: feelings about the traditions from which the different books arise. I had first thought to respond by trying to emphasize the strangeness, for us, of the Buddhist way of viewing death and life; but I realized, as I went on, that in many ways we seem more ready to receive the Buddhist teaching than, say, the teachings of Dante's *Divine Comedy*. It is Christianity that seems quaint and strange, the *New England Primer* being one particular manifestation of these qualities of an ancestral, perhaps antique, religion. We have a certain antipathy to the ancestral.

I might support my assertion with a disquisition on lower Manhattan in the 1970s, when, in the vagaries of national becoming, the Tibetan *Book of the Dead* seemed to manifest itself on the shelves of many of the hip bookstores, and on the metal sheets covering bathtubs in the kitchen-spaces of two-room apartments. It was common talk, then, to point out that someone, or the whole nation, was in the realm of Bardo. Yet the book meant, or hinted at, much more than that suggestive put-down. I felt then, and I feel now, that I know of nothing more beautiful and beckoning than certain parts, or even somewhat random parts, or in fact the sense of the existence, of the *Book of the Dead*. It has the authoritative wisdom not of an individual poem of the mind's becoming, such as Wordsworth's *Prelude*, but of a cosmic manual showing the mind to itself in images of a well-disposed and transhuman sagacity. And David has clarified for me the way in which it offers a transcendent gift—a text for inciting and directing the bereaved and burning imagination, inciting its life-force toward union with the death-journey of the departed. I wish I could go back and tell absent friends about how this book can be understood. We scarcely understood it at the time.

This idea of absent friends, and of coming toward an understanding of what one once had, or once did, or once might have done, offers a starting point for my response, which will make use of Dante's *Divine Comedy*. According to that idiosyncratic yet authoritative Christian book, a human being after death can expect to see absent friends again, and to understand his or her own life, and the friends' lives, and the lives of those who wrote the books of deepest communion— understand these in every detail and in essence, by seeing them in their relationship to the living, transcendent mystery—the relationship being one of origin and participation.

By contrast, at the heart of the Buddhist approach toward death— and life—is a deep letting-go: of individuality, of accomplishments, of precious moments to which one might say "stay awhile, you are so fair," of personal relationships. Highest of all concepts is the concept of emptiness which, as an experience rather than a concept, dissolves all concepts. The secret of secrets is that there is no such thing as a person. The ultimate concept is the ultimacy of the inconceivable. Life becomes permeated by the bright darkness of the child, in New England or Tibet, accepting sleep. Why does this seem more right or more satisfying to us today? Perhaps for us the concept of soul, and correspondingly the concept of our own souls, is thinning out.

In contrast with Buddhist emptiness as the goal in life and death, Dante describes a Cosmic Rose created by the divine light as it reflects off the highest sphere of the material world. It is a rose of distinct petals, composed of persons eternally alive, each in his or her proper place, their individual life experiences validated and transformed by expanding insight and love. If, in Buddhism, the awesomeness toward which we yearn is the peace of Nirvana, in Dante it is the will of a being-making God whose law, or even force, of love motivates beings. Not emptiness, but a fullness of being by way of a harmony of individuated beings.

Other contrasts derive from this essential one of maximum individuation vs. emptiness. At the first stage after death in the *Book of the Dead*, and at other stages thereafter, one has the opportunity, if one can make the proper choice, of merging with the pure light of consciousness, which in fact constitutes what one mistakenly identifies as oneself. In Dante, the divine is thought of as light—a similarity—but there is no possibility of an instant merging with the light. Rather, there is an educational process in which the individual soul becomes accustomed to more and more intense levels of light, being strengthened so that it will precisely not lose itself, will not be dazzled, but will eventually be able to gaze, for itself, into the purest and strongest light, the joy of which is that it is other than oneself. Is there, in the Buddhist tradition, at least for our minds, a secret appeal to self?

If, in the Tibetan *Book of the Dead*, one does not achieve a merging with the light, the process is one of increasing danger, of descent to lower and lower levels, the lowest level involving a kind of circling until one falls into rebirth. The motion of the *Divine Comedy* involves a circling, but its downward spiral through Hell leads, via a great reversal, to two upward spirals. *Purgatorio* and *Paradiso* together lead toward an increase, rather than a lessening, of understanding, and a reconciliation of contingency and absoluteness, not the destruction of one in the other.

Another striking difference has to do with the sense of hearing. One of the most effective aspects of the *Book of the Dead* is that, in the realm of Bardo, one hears sounds that transcend language, sounds that have to be endured precisely as transcendent. Pilgrims in the *Purgatorio* hear the singing of the words of the Mass or the Gospels with an ever-new understanding of their wider and wider meaning—an intensifying and expanding of significance rather than a swallowing of articulation in transcendent sound. Even more: In Dante's poem of the other world, there is much conversation. One meets not images of the mind's projections, but Cato himself, or Gabriel, most gallant of angels, or the lying Ulysses, the violent Vanni Fucci, the great ancestor Cacciaguida, or Casella, the talented friend of one's youth who set one's early poems to music. One runs into just about everybody on the way, and one's future after death depends on what one can learn from each.

By contrast, one of the magnificences of the *Book of the Dead* is the way in which the consciousness of the dead person is solitary in the cosmos which is behind its solitary illusions. No conversation is possible, though there may be the distant voices of those reading the text to its abandoned body. History is no longer important, only incidents of sheer recognition—or perhaps a better word is acceptance—of light and emptiness. In Dante, on the contrary, one's own history, and history itself, are what have to be understood. Only in Hell is one alone.

The ascent is mediated by others, each with their own story, quirks, particular avenues toward divinity. Recognition consists not in finding the cosmic meaning of solitude, but in recognizing that there are other individuals besides oneself, and that it is fellowship or community with them that embodies the divine.

Arriving at the lowest level in the *Book of the Dead*, circling and circling like the damned in Dante's Hell, the soul may be overwhelmed by the sweetness of the smell of a dung heap. I take this to be the craving for physical being, an overwhelming attraction to the smell of Aristotelian matter without form. It is sweet to exist, even as a pile of dung. This craving is part of Dante's doctrine—and paradox—in that he includes not release from individual material being or the rebirth into another body, but the resurrection of one's own physical body. All the individuals in Hell, Purgatory, and Heaven, will, in the most material sense, be themselves again, though perhaps not dung-creating selves. The implications of this are vast. Individual, physical, bodily existence is not *maya*, illusion, but the gift of God.

Professor Dennis Costa points out to his students that one of the ways Dante expresses this paradoxical doctrine of the resurrection of the body is by coining a word: *"transumanar,"* says Dante, is something that cannot be said in words.[1] Professor Costa says that Dante coined *"transumanar"* to express, gropingly, the mystery of the glorifying of a human being. The poet Dante's soul and perhaps body became something more than human which is yet the human destiny. And as the individual Dante is taken across to "his" divinity, the human itself is revealed as transcending itself, the transcendence enabled, subsumed, by the action of Christ, God become mortal man and risen, in the flesh, as immortal God/man. Dante's medieval doctrine of the body's eternity will later become Nietzsche's teaching about the coming of the *übermann*, who will transcend the human by passing through it, and who will achieve, among other things, a return to the body from the otherworldly soul. Nietzsche's Zarathustra says: "It was the sick and decaying who despised body and earth and invented the heavenly realm. . . . Ungrateful, these people deemed themselves transported from their bodies and this earth. But to whom did they owe the compulsions and raptures of their transport? To their bodies and this earth."[2]

I mention these things because I spoke earlier of the "transhuman sagacity" of the *Book of the Dead*; and "transhuman," one possible Anglicization of Dante's word, meant something very different in that context. Nietzsche's doctrine might be one way of measuring how different the transhuman is for Buddhism and for Dante. The Buddhist crossing, the Buddhist bridge through the human, leads to the dissolution of the body, thought of as a nexus of illusions; the other way, from Dante through Nietzsche, leads to the affirmation of the eternal recurrence of the self-same body. Nietzsche's words lead us to ask, at least, if there is respite in the Buddhist overcoming of body and earth.

The difference in the metaphysics of the *Book of the Dead* and Dante means that, if we read each properly, we read each differently from the other. For instance: in both books, the traveler must interpret the visual, the things that are seen. But what is important in the *Book of the Dead* is recognition that these are images. In Dante, time and again, the sights seen point to significance which tells us about created being as something of intrinsic worth which has been granted an ineffaceable reality. Each bit of being—even a shadow, a reed, a sparkle on the sea, the blood flowing out of a dying man's wound and blending with the swamp water—has an eternal significance and is of value because it happened, it existed.

These things being said, the *Divine Comedy* does teach something that seems, at least, rather Buddhist: remembering as letting-go. One must let go of those who have been one's friends and family but who have chosen evil. One must let go of friends who climb more slowly, or who have their own destinies to pursue. One must, and it hurts, let go of Vergil, the guide. One must let go of the love of one's life: We see the last look and smile of the woman Beatrice at the man Dante, across millions of miles of paradise, we hear her last harsh words judging Pope Boniface VIII in his hole in hell, and she turns away toward the divine light. It is a paradoxical moment of the most intense realization of self through others and the most intense turning of self toward what transcends all selves.

And we may say that, gazing deeper and deeper into the divine, Dante for a moment loses track of himself, of his ego, at the end of the *Paradiso*—but his will remains his, and he comes back to the world the most egotistical of Bodhisattvas, stamping his name on history as that great creator of illusions we admire as the artist. Dante's final teaching about the divine carries the paradox on. He takes the Buddhist image for the desires and dangers of life—namely, flame—and associates this with the divine principle, the love that moves the sun and the other stars. He compares God to three circles, and then sees something like a squaring of the circle—an image of God containing "our human effigy." This seems close to nonsense philosophically—Buddhist philosophy finds a much readier consistency in developing the doctrine of emptiness than Christianity does with the paradox of the human effigy intrinsic to the divine.

How do these differences play out in Western and Eastern attitudes toward death, and how it reflects back on life? In the Buddhist tradition, life is to be seen as something like process reality. When David Eckel says, "What I am now is just a flickering moment in the process of becoming something new. Life itself is a process of death and rebirth," we hear the note of Whitehead, although in Whitehead the particular manifestations of the process are not empty but have eternal value for God. In the Buddhist way of thinking, we are at every moment letting go, and have at the moment of death opportunities for an ultimate letting-go. The Western reaction, as it plays back into life, is more a grasping than a letting-go. One might recall resolution—an idea familiar from the thought of Heidegger and many others, going back to ancient ideas about fame and the Germanic word "deed," so close in sound to the word for "dead"—the idea that what one does in being-toward-death has a kind of eternity about it. As Dante sees it, soul and body survive, eternally, but are shaped in deathbound time; time cannot be canceled, and time is the playing out of indelible truth. Thus among Dante's metaphors for ultimate reality is a book: a coherent, inexpungable record of everything that has happened between birth and death.[3] To put it another way, we might say that the *Book of the Dead*, or Buddhism as characterized by David Eckel, describes death as the opportunity to use one's knowledge, whereas the *Divine Comedy* describes death as part of an ongoing educative process.

In both versions, the moment of death, the moment evoked in the magnificent child's prayer which is the seed of our meditations, marks a crucial change. The invoking of the Buddha Amitābha at the moment of death has a kind of counterpart in Dante's presentation of last-minute repentance. And again, the similarity points to a profound difference. Repentance in Dante does not bring about a merging with the divine consciousness, but rather a true regret for the actual life one has lived, for its doneness, and an overwhelming desire to understand it and to be chastened and forgiven for it, in order to truly become—oneself. It is the first in a series of stages of the recovery of self.

This recovery of the self in Dante involves, unlike the *Book of the Dead*, a looking-back. At a crucial moment in the *Paradiso*, Dante looks back toward the "savage little threshing floor" that is the earth seen from the verge of the material world.[4] He sees, and turns away. It may, at first, remind one of a Buddhist moment. Life is viewed, here, with detachment, contempt, horror, calm, something like the joy of *moksha* or liberation. But this moment in Dante's consciousness has a future: it is taken as a step toward viewing life harmoniously as a great communion across all of time and space. And this harmony must include the taking seriously of how each of us has lived in this savage place with its opportunity to earn our names and selves.

One can feel the profundity and strangeness of the Buddhist perspective by realizing that, from its point of view, the names Thermopylae, Salamis, Normandy, and the helmeted men and boys who, for their reasons, did deeds there, are the cricket chirping under the helmet in Basho's poem. The deaths, courage, cowardice, kindness, savagery, and the things thereby preserved or enabled, were illusory. Repeating the names is as natural and evanescent and, in its way, meaningless and sorrowful, and sorrowfully meaningless, and meaninglessly sorrowful, as the singing of a cricket. Similarly, are the nobility and handsomeness of the Buddha/deer in the Jātaka tale, and the plea of the pregnant doe, illusions?—not deeds, nor great and humble presences, but pointers toward renunciations of self, useful little bridges toward the ultimate mercy of nonbeing? As such, then, not noble except as they contribute to the ultimate negation of the illusion of nobility?

I find it hard to think so. Having admitted my deep attraction to the *Book of the Dead*, I ought also to admit that my review of Dante has shaken somewhat the ease and pleasure with which I thought to approach again that luminous presence of my early twenties, and has thrown some bitterness into the sweetness to be expected, and found, there. Western questions trouble the mind, and the moral sense: What if being is not the sweet smell of dung, but a gift of the sacred? What if what we do is not recycled, but remembered? What if we are, ultimately, not a spark of pure consciousness but a communing soul, made by and making others? What if our attraction to the East carries with it the danger of a mere lapse from what it most behooves us to live by? What if the horror and guilt which, as we look at the recent history of the West, we seek to overcome or avoid, are properly to be confronted as body and soul rather than as epiphenomena? What if we really are doing what we are doing, and only in that realization does there lie any hope of more good and less evil? Most strangely for us, perhaps, what if the child's prayer "If I should die before I wake / I pray the Lord my soul to take"—a prayer whose premise is, in many parts of the world, all too frequently true—might, in its petition as well as its premise, offer a glimpse, granted to us, not manufactured by us, of reality?

NOTES

1. Dante *Paradiso* Canto 1.70.
2. Friedrich Nietzsche, *Thus Spoke Zarathustra*, trans. Walter Kaufmann (New York: Penguin Press, 1954; reprint ed.1978), p. 32.
3. Dante *Paradiso* 33.86.
4. Dante *Paradiso* 22.21.

Why People in Stories Choose Mortality When They Could Have Immortality

WENDY DONIGER

PEOPLE CHOOSE mortality in myths in two different but closely related ways: sometimes they choose to *have* a mortal partner (and therefore, usually, to be mortal themselves), and sometimes they choose, more directly, to *be* mortal themselves.[1] Let us begin with people who choose mortal partners, and move on to consider people who choose death.

WHY CHOOSE A MORTAL PARTNER?

The myths of choice send several different messages: some of their protagonists prefer their own kind, but others prefer creatures from another world. Certain patterns prevail in one culture, others in others. But statistical generalizations are never very sound and seldom even interesting. There are four paradigms: (1) human men who prefer human women, (2) nonhuman women who prefer human men, (3) nonhuman men who prefer human women, and (4) human women who prefer human men. Let us consider them one by one, beginning with (1) human men who prefer human women.

At the very beginning of the *Odyssey*, Odysseus rejects Calypso. When we first meet Odysseus he is longing for his homecoming and his wife, but the powerful nymph Calypso, the bright goddess, keeps him back in her hollow caves, longing to make him her husband.[2] Later, when Calypso expresses her disbelief that he should prefer his mortal wife to her, an immortal woman, he replies:

> Mighty goddess, don't be angry with me because of this. I know perfectly well that the thoughtful Penelope is not as good as you

103

are to look at, in appearance or stature, for she is a mortal and you are not merely immortal, but ageless. Yet even so I wish and hope every day to come home and to see the day of my homecoming.[3]

And with that, he goes to bed with Calypso. Nothing is said in Penelope's favor other than the fact that she is a part of a home. All else is against her: she lacks beauty, size, immortality, and youth. Setting aside the fact that the man of many wiles would not make the mistake of praising other women to the woman he is sleeping with at the moment, as Zeus does to his wife Hera,[4] what endears Penelope to Odysseus is her *lack* of divine characteristics.

Calypso offers Odysseus an immortal body; this is death-in-life, for Calypso is, as her name tells us, the one who veils, resonant with the black cloud of death that veils mortals.[5] Odysseus has already experienced the insubstantiality of life-in-death during his previous encounter, in the land of the dead, with the shade of another woman: his mother. Three times he attempts to hold her, but she flutters out of his hands like a shadow or a dream, and tells him, significantly, to tell his wife about his experience among the dead.[6] There, too, Odysseus encounters Achilles, the man who was *almost* immortal (which is, perhaps, as meaningless as its opposite: being a little bit pregnant), and who insists that he would rather work in the fields as a slave than be king over all the dead.[7] Odysseus, therefore, knows precisely what he is keeping and what he is giving up when he turns Calypso down.

Odysseus is not alone. To select just three famous instances, Gilgamesh in the *Gilgamesh Epic* rejects Ishthar; the human hero Arjuna, in the *Mahabharata*, rejects the immortal nymph Urvashi[8] (a story that may actually have historical connections with the tale of Odysseus's rejection of Calypso);[9] and Ovid's Cephalus rejects Aurora.[10] Men often reject goddesses, though usually when the goddess is depicted as a whore. Many texts depict this rejection, though few actually give positive reasons for the human man's preference for human women.

The mortal man who rejects the nonhuman woman is just half of a broader paradigm, of which the other half is supplied by (2) the nonhuman woman who seeks the mortal man. Why do nonhuman women, like Calypso—for a while—choose human men? Different cultures suggest different reasons. Often, the otherworldly woman chooses life when she chooses her mortal lover. In Christian mythology it is the mortals who are ultimately immortal—for they have immortal souls, which is what the nonhuman women want.[11] In order to get their own souls, these women do not always take the men's souls away (though some do); it usually suffices just to seduce them. Undine, the water nymph, is such an otherworldly, immortal creature. She is best known from Friedrich de la Motte Fouqué's German novella *Undine*, which later inspired an opera by E. T. A. Hoffmann and many plays (one by Jean Giraudoux) and movies (one with Audrey Hepburn), as well as Hans Christian Andersen's story "The Little Mermaid." Fouqué stressed not the bestiality but the otherworldliness of the heroine; the hero is the one who proves to be morally bestial, as he abandons Undine and destroys her. The human lover of Giraudoux's *Ondine* betrays her with the lost (human) daughter of the human parents who had adopted Ondine, the woman for whom Ondine is in a sense a changeling; and, though she tries to save him, he dies for betraying her, in keeping with the inexorable contract enforced by her father. The issue of the soul is given a nice twist in a discussion between Ondine and a human queen about her likely betrayal by her human lover. Queen: "He has a small soul." Ondine: "I haven't got any soul, that's much worse." Queen: "The question doesn't arise for you, or for any creatures except humans. The world's soul breathes in and out through every bird and fish and animal; but man wanted his soul to himself. So, like a fool, he chopped up the human spirit into bits so that every man could have one. . . ."[12] This Ondine has no soul but apparently does very well without one, while her human lover, who presumably has one, dies and presumably loses his soul.

The idea that the woman from the otherworld seeks not the body of her mortal lover but her own soul from him can be traced back to Paracelsus' treatise on the four nature spirits. One of these is an Undine, who resembles a human woman in every way except the possession of a soul, which she obtains only if she unites with a man. And so, Paracelsus tells us, she seduces a man in secret, just as a heathen seeks baptism in order to get a soul and to find eternal life as a Christian.[13] Paracelsus went on to condemn Mélusine, a serpent woman who masqueraded as a human woman, though never on Saturday; when her husband violated his promise and intruded upon her in her Saturday bath, he discovered Mélusine, "her lower extremities changed into the tail of a monstrous fish or serpent." He cursed her: "Away, hateful serpent, contaminator of my honorable race!" She kissed him and embraced him for the last time, then swept from the room, "leaving the impression of her foot on the stone she last touched." She returned in a ghostly form at night to nurse at her breast the two babies that she had left behind.[14] (Heinrich Heine is said to have remarked that Mélu-sine's husband was a relatively happy man, since his wife was only *half* a snake.[15]) Later Christian mythology, polluted by the twin forces of racism and sexism, assimilated the soulless pagans to both women and Jews. And Otto Weininger, a Jew who committed suicide in 1903, "set out to prove that all Jews were, essentially, women. 'Those who have no soul can have no craving for immortality, and so it is with the woman and the Jew.'"[16] Were mermaids Jews longing to be Christians, or just women longing to have what men had?

The third paradigm, (3) the story of the nonhuman man who prefers a human woman, is typified by Zeus, whose many affairs with human women plagued Greek mythology (and his wife Hera). More broadly, the mating of male gods with human women is one of the dominant themes of worldwide mythology; it was a popular Christian theme as well (think for instance of the Holy Spirit and Mary), in part because of the arguments just cited for the superiority of the human soul. Kierkegaard, in his analysis of the Danish tale of Agnete and the merman, perhaps under the influence of the paradigm of Undine, merely switched the genders and suggested that the winning of a human soul was the reason for the merman's desire for Agnete: "The merman does not want to seduce Agnete although he has seduced many others. He is no merman any more. . . . Yet he knows . . . that he can be saved by the love of an innocent maiden. . . . Soon he was tired of Agnete, yet her body was never found."[17]

But the non-Christian texts themselves give a nongendered rea-son for the nonhumans' preference for humans, one rather different from the reason constructed for them by Christian texts: they desire a child rather than a soul. In the Scandinavian myths of the seal-men, "the essential plot concerns the desire of the seal for contact with the human world and for a son."[18] In many mythologies, immortals do not have children because if one doesn't die there is no need to reproduce oneself. This explains why gods seduce and impregnate mortal women rather than just desiring them or seeking their sexual pleasure among them. The story of the loss of Eden in the Hebrew Bible presents the causal sequence in the opposite order: because there is sex there will be death. This is the logic that operates in many mythologies to hold women responsible for death, because they are responsible for birth.

Gregory Nagy stated the case very well for the Greek gods: "As we see clearly from the Hesiodic *Theogony*, the lineage of purebred

Olympian gods comes to a halt, for all practical purposes, at the third generation. . . . The Olympian gods of the third generation propagate by mating with mortals, not with each other. Mortal genes, as it were, are dominant, while immortal ones are recessive, in that any element of mortality in a lineage produces mortal offspring."[19] Is the choice of a mortal lover a move from Eros to Thanatos? I think not; on the contrary, as we have just seen, death, or rather mortality, is what makes sex possible. Roberto Calasso suggests a rather different reason for the (Greek) gods' preference for human women, a reason also highly meaningful in our broader context: "When it came to his amorous adventures, Zeus found mortal women far more attractive. He wasn't interested in bothering those figures of fate; they were too similar to one another, disturbing the way twins can be, too ancient, and, in the end, hostile."[20] Unlike human women with their asymmetrical flaws, all goddesses in their perfection look alike.[21]

Paradigm (4), a human woman who prefers a human man, is well exemplified by Damayanti, the heroine of an ancient story told in the Sanskrit Epic, the *Mahabharata*, who chooses her mortal husband over four gods who wish to marry her and who impersonate him, apparently perfectly. But she loves her human husband with all his imperfections and recognizes him by the imperfections that she loves: sweaty, blinking, earth-bound, dusty, shadowy old Nala.[22] In Robert Johnson's Jungian analysis of Damayanti,

> She chooses—that is, she maintains a realistic human perspective when she is offered a god as a husband. . . . She avoids the romantic fantasy of a god as a lover. . . . She is aware of limits and chooses the limited human, who needs to blink his eyes, over the divine, which would be timeless and immortal. She is capable of seeing that the human condition is preferable to the divine at a particular point in her life. . . . Women in their relationships with men often feel that the men disappear psychologically and emotionally. This ability to identify one small sign of a man's true nature and connect with it can help him toward wholeness.[23]

Yes, well, though there is little to disagree with in this analysis, it hardly does justice to the issues raised in the myth. In a Sanskrit text, Damayanti far more eloquently states the reasons why a mortal might spurn a god:

Indra's merits, though attractive, do not make me give up a man who pleases me. People are unwilling to give up the three worldly goals of life—pleasure, religion, and profit—inferior though they are to [the fourth, transcendent goal,] Release. I will marry the immortal Indra—in his mortal form as king Nala. Even a virtuous man must come down from heaven [when he uses up his *karma*], but when he departs from here [at death], he goes to heaven. The two types of future are like gravel and sugar.[24]

In Hindu mythology, the gods are twenty-five years old forever.[25] To some of us over fifty, this might appear an attractive alternative; but to most of us, it would not.

Barbara Fass Leavy has speculated on the reasons why human women in folklore and myth "spurn the advances of demon lovers, preferring reality to the imagined pleasures of the otherworld"[26] (though her remarks also apply to men who reject goddesses):

> Of primary importance is the nature of the otherworld itself, a land of dreams-come-true, where man is forever young and pleasures forever available. It is a static realm, lacking the earthly cycles of birth and death, a point worth stressing, for if the otherworld is, as the Irish put it, the Land of the Living, that is, a world in which no one dies, it also appears that it is a world in which no one is born. . . . La Belle Dame sans Merci and the land in which she dwells are not creative. What they supply instead is perpetual bliss, and bliss, when it is its own end, inevitably palls.[27]

Endless light and clarity are exhausting (as we learn from those who have experienced the White Nights of summer in Stockholm or Leningrad).

Angela Carter, in her retelling of "Beauty and the Beast," has imagined the heroine's reasons for rejecting divine perfection when she contemplates her divine beast:

> I never saw a man so big look so two-dimensional. . . . He throws our human aspirations to the godlike sadly awry, poor fellow; only from a distance would you think The Beast not much different from any other man, although he wears a mask with a man's face painted most beautifully on it. Oh, yes, a beautiful face; but one with too much formal symmetry of feature to be entirely human: one profile of his mask is the mirror image of the other, too perfect, uncanny. . . .[28]

The god who may become the mirror image of the human whom he impersonates (as the Hindu gods impersonate Nala for Damayanti) is himself his own mirror image, too perfect and symmetrical to be real. The mirror here makes possible a symmetry and perfection that is inhuman. Here we may recall that the makers of Persian carpets deliberately introduce a flaw into each carpet as a sign of humility and in order to avoid the hubris of attempted perfection.

The choice made in these stories is the choice of real life, however brief, in preference to infinite non-life, misleadingly referred to as immortality. The logic behind these apparently "wrong" choices is one that opts for a kind of continuous connectedness [29] which is our symbolic immortality, the fragile, ephemeral, conditional, dependent intensity of real life, the emotional chiaroscuro,[30] the sense of impending loss that makes what we have so precious while we have it, more precious than the security of an eternity without that immediacy and intensity. To choose the imperfect mortal instead of the perfect immortal is to accept and even affirm one's own mortality and insufficiency, rejecting the vain goal of attaching one's perishable self to some seemingly perfect and unchanging unearthly form. Goddesses often desire mortal men, and gods mortal women, because of the heightened sexuality and excitement of those who change and suffer. Immortality in this view is not an expansion of being human, but a diminution or denial of being human; gods are less rather than more than human. Heraclitus may have had this in mind when he said, "Immortals mortal, mortals immortal; [immortals] living the death of these; [mortals] dying the life of the others."[31] That is, the life of the gods is like our death; and our apparent death is both the price and the value of our life.

The paradox that underlies these myths is the belief that to choose a mortal lover is to choose life (either in the form of an immortal soul or in the form of truly vivid existence), while to choose an immortal is not, as one might think, to choose life, let alone immortality, but to choose death, for the man who falls in love with a goddess often dies as a consequence. Thus the myth of death meets itself coming in at the door: women choose mortal husbands and death, while men who choose immortal wives also inadvertently choose death. To put it differently, goddesses bring death to mortal men, while human women choose death (for themselves and also for mortal men). In either case, it is the female who appears to be responsible for death.

(A female—not his lover but his mother—was responsible for the Achilles' heel of Achilles. His mother, the goddess Thetis, held him by the heel when she dipped him into the waters that made the rest of him immortal; the heel was the place where—because she forgot to dip it, too—he remained vulnerable and through which death entered him.)

Stepping outside the text for a moment, we might suggest that since on the one hand our texts were composed by human men and on the other the superiority of human men over gods is by no means obvious, it is hardly surprising that the preference for human men inspires a great deal of fancy ideological footwork of justification in our myths. One of the many functions of a myth is to affirm the status quo (or more precisely, what David Tracy has called the fluxus quo[32]). The myths in which the woman chooses a mortal husband combine the choice of her own role with the choice of her own mortality and thus doubly affirm the fluxus quo. When our stories imagine that a human might be able to make love with a god, they do so in order to encourage readers or hearers to imagine that they would rather keep the human spouses that they have.

WHY CHOOSE DEATH?

Similarly, many Hindu myths imagine what the world was like when there was no death, in order to affirm either that we must settle for what we have (since it is our own fault that death came into the world),[33] or that we really would not be happy if there were no death (there would be overcrowding, no moral law, etc.).[34] The tribal mythologies of India also deal with the theme of overcrowding; as Verrier Elwin remarks, "The notion that if nobody died the world would become overcrowded and unable to support the population is widely distributed."[35] A typical example of such a myth appears among the Rengma Nagas: At first there was no day and night, and the dead lived in the same world as the living. God had to divide day and night, so that the dead would work at night, and he moved the dead "to another world, too, for when the dead and the living lived in the same world they were so numerous that there was danger of there not being enough land."[36] The Hindu belief in the need for differentiation of all kinds, between day and night as well as mortal and immortal, the need for a separate place for each group, combines here with the motif of overcrowding.

Tribal myths also recognize other positive aspects of mortality: At first there was no death, but there was old age; the old men asked God for death, and then everyone—even some young people—died.[37] The implication here is that death is a mixed blessing: it is better than old age, but it is not welcome to the young. This ambivalence toward death is also found among the Toda:

> Mirth in Funeral
> At first no Toda died. After a time a Piedr man died. (At the funeral, some people wept, but others danced and sang. The goddess Teikirzi, seeing the people weeping,) took pity and came to bring the dead man back to life. (But then she saw that some people seemed quite happy, and she decided not to raise the dead man. Then she decreed that at funerals some would weep, while others would be happy.)[38]

Here we are left to imagine why some would weep while others would experience what Shakespeare's Claudius argued for, "mirth in funeral."[39]

In a story from the ninth-century Chinese *Sequel to the Record of Dark Mysteries*, an old man tells Du Zichun to remain silent and unmoved through illusions of pain and suffering, as he brews an elixir of immortality in a cauldron. Du Zichun experiences the illusion that he is reborn as a woman and gives birth to a son, but when her husband dashes their two-year old child to the ground and kills him, Du Zichun, full of love and attachment, forgets his vow and cries out involuntarily, "Ah!" thus losing his chance for immortality. As Wei-Yi Li points out, this story confronts the reader with the problem of inhuman immortality, an enlightenment that implies the denial of being human. We empathize with Du Zichun's failure, because had he not cried out, had he successfully divested himself of all forms of attachment, he would have behaved inhumanly.[40] A close Greek parallel to this Chinese story is offered by the story of Demeter, who, after the descent into the underworld of her own child, Persephone, came in disguise as a nurse in order to make the child of a human king and queen immortal; but the child's mother entered just when Demeter was dipping the child in fire. She cried out, making Demeter stop before the job was finished. She could not stand the inhumanity it takes to become immortal.[41] When Giraudoux's Jupiter offers Alcmena immortality for herself, she refuses it and says, "It's a sort of betrayal for a human to become immortal. Besides, when I think of the perfect rest death will give us from all our little tirednesses and third-rate sorrows, I'm grateful to it for its fullness, its bounty even."[42]

DEATH MAKES AN OFFER WE CANNOT REFUSE

Other texts express the closely related theme of the apparently *inadvertent* choice of mortality, a choice often made as the result of a trick or a riddle. This is the point of an Indonesian myth cited by Sir James George Frazer:

> The Stone and the Banana
> The natives of Poso, a district of Central Celebes, say that in the beginning the sky was very near the earth, and that the Creator, who lived in it, used to let down his gifts to men at the end of a rope. One day he thus lowered a stone; but our first father and mother would have none of it and they called out to their Maker, "What have we to do with this stone? Give us something else." The Creator complied and hauled away at the rope; the stone mounted up and up until it vanished from sight. Presently the rope was seen coming down from heaven again, and this time there was a banana at the end of it instead of a stone. Our first parents ran at the banana and took it. Then there came a voice from heaven saying, "Because ye have chosen the banana, your life shall be like its life. When the banana-tree has offspring, the parent stem dies; so shall ye die and your children shall step into your place. Had ye chosen the stone, your life would have been like the life of the stone changeless and immortal." The man and his wife mourned over their fatal choice, but it was too late; that is how through the eating of a banana death came into the world.[43]

They chose the banana because it was luscious (and perhaps phallic), a symbol of life, while the stone was a symbol of death. But in making this choice they foolishly and unwittingly threw away their chance of being immortal, never changing, like the stone. The stone is the touchstone, as it were, in contests between gods pretending to be human (who can lift the heavier stone?), contests in which the stone (in implicit contrast with flesh or a banana) represents the deity. But were humans in fact so foolish in choosing, instead of the sterility of an eternity of stone, the luscious, phallic banana of death? Did they really make the "wrong" choice? They made the same choice that Damayanti made in preferring Nala over Indra, sugar over gravel (that is, banana over stone). By choosing death (the banana, the mortal), you choose life (rather than sterility), and by choosing immortality (life with a goddess), you end up choosing death (she kills you).

Prometheus made the same choice for humankind: the flesh, instead of the smoke. Operating on behalf of humans, Prometheus thinks that he tricks Zeus into choosing bones wrapped in skin, while mortals get the meat of the sacrificial animal; Zeus, however, thinks that he has tricked Prometheus into choosing meat, which rots and dies, while the gods live on the smoke of the oblation, which lasts forever. [44] We might think that Prometheus outsmarts himself by engineering the choice that makes humans mortal and gods immortal. On the other hand, we might think that Prometheus had the last word after all, tricking the trickster: for he procured for us mortals a life of change and the delicious taste of food, a life in the flesh, rather than the shadowy existence of smoke that drove Zeus to find his sexual pleasures among mortal women. Here we may also recall that Zeus himself was replaced by a stone in the belly of his mother in order to foil the filicidal impulses of his father, Cronos;[45] here too there was a choice between a stone that fooled the god (like the bones that did or did not fool Zeus) and the flesh, or the banana, that survived: Zeus himself.

Plato, in the *Gorgias* (494b), writes of the contrast between a stone and a certain bird, the *charadria*, who constantly eats and urinates. To compare the life of pleasure to the life of happiness, he says, is like comparing the *charadria* to a stone; is happiness just scratching an itch? The ridiculous bird through whom water (and presumably food) passes constantly takes the place of the banana in the Indonesian myth, or, closer to home, the flesh in the myth of Prometheus (or the child Zeus in the myth of the foiling of Cronos). (Lévi-Strauss wrote of similar myths about the goat-sucker, a South American bird that defecates constantly.[46]) Is Plato here making fun of these mythologies of choice and contrast, even making fun of the myth of Prometheus and Zeus? I wonder.

Carlo Ginzburg cites another variant of the Indonesian story of the banana from the island of Ceram (Molucca):

The stone wanted men to have only one arm, one leg, one eye, and be immortal; the banana tree wanted them to have two arms, two legs, two eyes and to be able to procreate. The banana tree won the dispute: but the stone insisted that men be subject to death. The myth invites us to recognize symmetry as a characteristic of human beings.[47]

Symmetry—or duality, I would say. Yet most of these stories are arguing for just the opposite, for *asymmetry*, imperfection, as the defining human characteristic. And the two legs, regarded as standing in opposition not to one leg but to four, function as the sign not of symmetry but rather of non-animal mortality.

The wrong choice that the women, or, sometimes, men, make turns out to be the right choice after all—the *felix culpa*, the fortunate error that makes human life possible. A beautiful Aynu variant of this myth contrasts the stone with wood rather than fruit, blames a presumably male animal rather than a human woman, and elaborates upon a whole series of fortunate errors:

The Stone and the Otter
     When Kotankarukamui set out to make humans, he sent a sparrow to ask the heavenly deities what they thought he should use to make them. They replied that wood/trees would be good (and sent back the sparrow). Later they thought that stone would in fact be a more durable material and summoned the otter and dispatched him with great urgency to the lower world to pass on this (new) command to Kotankarukamui. However, on his way Otter was distracted by a large school of fish and concentrating his whole attention on catching the fish completely forgot his mission, thus delivering his message far too late. Thus it was that humans were made of trees and not a single person is saved from aging and perishing. Yet, humans are also born one after another, they grow and develop and multiply. This too occurs because of the otter's forgetfulness. The deity was angry at Otter for this and stamped on his head; that is why it is so flat even today. Others say that the tree used to make humans was a willow and thus it is that humans, like the willow, bend and quiver as they age.[48]

Humans do not have a choice here: their fate is decided through the mistakes of two other actors, the gods (who choose the wrong substance at first, and wait too long to correct their error) and the otter (who miscarries his message, a common theme in cosmogonies). The stone is contrasted explicitly with the wood but also implicitly with the otter, whose playfulness and forgetfulness are eminently human. This text also makes explicit what was won as well as what was lost: the pleasures of growing and multiplying (that is, the pleasures of the otter); even old age is depicted by an image of grace and beauty, the willow.

The choice of death is not conscious in these myths; it is the result of a trick or a mistake, usually associated with food (but not always: the Aynu story of the otter imagines the choice as between building materials). The food itself may be what causes the unwitting mortal to make the unconscious choice of mortality; recall how Persephone ate the pomegranate and was doomed to remain half the year in the world of the dead and half the year among the living.[49] There is also a widespread folk belief that the human who eats fairy food must remain in the other world. A corollary of this belief occurs in the Hindu story of Naciketas, who did *not* eat anything in the underworld and thereby forced Death to tell him the secret of mortality and immortality.[50] And then there was that business in Eden, when Eve too chose the fruit (an apple? a banana?), and sex, and death.

SLOUGHING OFF IMMORTALITY

The skin-sloughing quality of the snake is not mentioned but remains implicit in the story of Eden; it becomes explicit in an entire, related corpus of non-Christian mythologies. In some variants of this myth, the sloughing of the skin—a major ingredient in the modern face-lift that is meant to restore youth—brings not youth but death. Frazer cites a variant from the Central Celibes:

The Grandmother Who Sloughed Her Skin
In old times men, like serpents and shrimps, had the power of casting their skin whereby they became young again. There was an old woman who had a grandchild. Now the old woman went to the water to bathe and she hung her old skin upon a tree. When she returned to the house her grandchild kept saying: "You are not my grandmother, my grandmother was old and you are young." Then the old woman went back to the water and drew on her old skin again.[51]

The women fight about the surface, the skin, but what is at stake runs far deeper—death. Frazer cites other myths very like this one, including one fetchingly entitled, "The Composite Story of the Perverted Message and the Cast Skin." Another story in this series was recorded in 1909:

The Young Mother
To Kabinana and To Karvuvu are brothers. Their mother had cast her skin and now she was a young girl once more. But To Karvuvu cried he would not have his mother like this and he brought her old skin back again. To Kabinana said: "Why have you put the old skin back again on our mother? Now the serpents will cast their skin and our descendants will die!"[52]

Several other versions, from Tanna in New Hebrides and the Admiralty Islands, also depict a son who rejects his mother when she sheds her skin ("I don't know you. . . . You are not my mother").[53] In retrospect, we can see that the version from the Celibes simultaneously distances and exaggerates the problem by making the older woman not a mother but a grandmother, and erases the overtones of incest by making the younger person not a son but a daughter. The psychoanalytical anthropologist Geza Roheim glosses these stories for us: "A child or grandchild refuses to recognize the rejuvenated grandmother or mother in the young woman. In the last version quoted above and belonging to this group the difficulty lies in the Oedipus complex. If mothers were to cast their skins and hence mankind were to live forever, sons would want their mothers for their wives—hence we must die."[54] The face-lift confuses the generations in such a way as to foster incest.

Malinowski recorded a related myth from the Trobriand Islands which spells out, at least in Malinowski's retellings, the implications for the origins of death:

The Animals of the Below and the Above
After a span of spiritual existence in Tuma, the nether world, an individual grows old, grey, and wrinkled; and then he has to rejuvenate by sloughing his skin. Even so did human beings in the old primeval times, when they lived underground. When they first came to the surface, they had not yet lost this ability; men and women could live eternally young.

They lost the faculty, however, by an apparently trivial, yet important and fateful event. Once upon a time there lived in the village of Bwadela an old woman who dwelt with her daughter and granddaughter; three generations of genuine matrilineal descent. The grandmother and granddaughter went out one day to bathe in the tidal creek. The girl remained on the shore, while the old woman went away some distance out of sight. She took off her skin, which, carried by the tidal current, floated along the creek until it stuck on a bush. Transformed into a young girl, she came back to her granddaughter. The latter did not recognize her; she was afraid of her, and bade her begone. The old woman, mortified and angry, went back to her bathing place, searched for her old skin, put it on again, and returned to her granddaughter. This time she was recognized and thus greeted: "A young girl came here; I was afraid; I chased her away." Said the grandmother: "No, you didn't want to recognize me. Well, you will become old—I shall die." They went home to where the daughter was preparing the meal. The old woman spoke to her daughter: "I went to bathe; the tide carried my skin away; your daughter did not recognize me; she chased me away. I shall not slough my skin. We shall all become old. We shall all die."

After that men lost the power of changing their skin and of remaining youthful. The only animals who have retained the power of changing the skin are the "animals of the below"—snakes, crabs, iguanas, and lizards: this is because men also once lived under the ground. These animals come out of the ground and they still can change their skin. Had men lived above, the "animals of the above"—birds, flying-foxes, and insects—would also be able to change their skins and renew their youth.[55]

This variant blames women, as usual, for death and goes on to divide the blame between the foolish young woman and the vindictive old woman (the mother, cited in the beginning, vanishes, leaving the generations on both sides to fight it out); in an attempt to solve the problem of old age, the women inadvertently invent death. The disguised grandmother in this story might lead us to view the story of Red Riding Hood in a new light, not as a conflict between the kindly granny and the wicked old wolf, but as a conflict within granny herself, who has her own big teeth with which to devour her little granddaughter.

Another Indonesian myth also connects the inadvertent choice of death with the sloughing of the skin:

The Origin of Death

The wise and ancient Ndangi Lawo lived a long life amidst plenty by following the "word" or teachings of the Mother and Father Creator. Like all people back then, he would never die, because every time he would get old, he would shed his skin like a snake, be "renewed," and become young again. The Sun and Moon, however, would never set, and as a result, the earth would get very hot. So a young man named Mbora Pyaku went to the Creator to request that the Sun and Moon be permitted to set from time to time to cool things off. The creator agreed to let the Sun and Moon "live and die and live again," as Mbora Pyaku requested, but in exchange, "when humans die, they will die forever."

As soon as Mbora Pyaku thus changed the "word" of the ancestors, Ndangi Lawo died, and people first began to cry and weep. Children began to be born, and people began to reckon time, counting the "months and years" until they died.[56]

Thus, death came into the world—from the confusion of the idea that the Sun is too hot and must have periodic times off (temporary death) with the idea that mortals made the mistaken choice to have non-periodic time off (permanent death).

CONCLUSION

Most of us do not assume that our ancestors chose death for the human race; we assume that it is one of the givens of human existence. Some indeed, including some doctors and scientists, believe that immortality is even now a real goal, not yet realized; and others strive to ward off death, as if forever, through the magic of the Nautilus machine, the face-lift, the weird diets, the younger and younger lovers.

Nor do all mythologies assume that we chose or choose death, or, on the other hand, that we choose non-death. Virgil's Aeneas, visiting the dead as Odysseus had done, asks his father if the dead really wish to undergo the torment of rebirth, and learns that the dead have no choice at all: though each of us suffers his or her own Hell, the gods erase everyone's memories so that they begin to wish that they had bodies again.[57]

We might therefore ask why so many authors from so many different cultures have found it useful to imagine that we once had a choice about death, and chose to die. It is not just a matter of wishful thinking, though this plays a part. Nor is it just a matter (though this, too, plays a part) of de-dichotomizing our normally Cartesian way of thinking, a matter of learning, as Lao-tzu so nicely put it, that "is and isn't produce one another,"[58] that the reality of death must be balanced by the idea of non-death, that life and death define one another. Rather, I think that mythmakers award themselves, and their readers/hearers, a kind of retrospective empowerment that prefers even the guilt of bearing responsibility for the loss of immortality through either a wrong choice or a stupid error to the indignity of utter helplessness in the face of death. "Rage, rage against the dying of the light," writes Dylan Thomas, but these myths decant that rage into a fantasy that allows us to tell ourselves that we are, as an earlier poet, William Ernest Henley put it, captains of our souls, masters of our fate.[59]

The *conscious* preference for the human that we find in this mythology explains one of the enduring mysteries of the American cinema: Why did Dorothy want to leave Oz and return to Kansas? This decision always bothered me (I am a New Yorker, with a New Yorker's scorn for everything west of the Hudson), and I was not surprised to learn that it bothered the author himself, who later reworked the story. For in subsequent Oz books by L. Frank Baum, as Salman Rushdie tells us,

> Dorothy, ignoring the "lessons" of the ruby slippers, went back to Oz, in spite of the efforts of Kansas folk, including Auntie Em and Uncle Henry, to have her dreams brainwashed out of her . . . ; and, in the sixth book of the series, she took Auntie Em and Uncle Henry with her, and they all settled down in Oz, where Dorothy became a Princess. So Oz finally *became* home; the imagined world became the actual world.[60]

But mythology all over the word offers many precedents for Dorothy's original preference for a real home over the seductive world of fantasy, the world of immortality.

The poet William Butler Yeats, in "The Stolen Child," his retelling of the folktale of the fairy changeling, simultaneously tells us why one might choose the fairy world, and what one would lose by that choice:

> Where the wave of moonlight glosses
> The dim grey sands with light,
> Far off by furthest Rosses
> We foot it all the night,
> Weaving olden dances,
> Mingling hands and mingling glances
> Till the moon has taken flight;
> To and fro we leap
> And chase the frothy bubbles,
> While the world is full of troubles
> And is anxious in its sleep.
> Come away, O human child!
> To the waters and the wild
> With a faery, hand in hand,
> For the world's more full of weeping
> than you can understand.
>
> . . . .
>
> Away with us he's going,
> The solemn-eyed:
> He'll hear no more the lowing
> Of the calves on the warm hillside
> Or the kettle on the hob
> Sing peace into his breast,
> Or see the brown mice bob
> Round and round the oatmeal-chest.
> For he comes, the human child,
> To the waters and the wild
> With a faery, hand in hand,
> From a world more full of weeping
> than he can understand.[61]

The world is full of troubles, anxious in its sleep, full of weeping. The child throws all of this away without understanding it, but the poet misses, on the child's behalf, the things that make human life precious: the sounds (the lowing of the calves and the singing of the kettle), the visions (the brown mice bobbing round the oatmeal-chest), and the warmth of the sun.

NOTES

1. The first few pages of this essay are based upon an earlier discussion of the same theme in another context, in my *Splitting the Difference: Gender and Myth in Ancient Greece and India*; the rest of the essay develops the theme in a different direction. I am also indebted to Stephanie Nelson, whose insightful response to a presentation of this essay in April, 2000, led to several fruitful revisions.

2. Homer *Odyssey* 1.13–15. All references are to the A. T. Murray translation (Cambridge, Mass.: Loeb Library, 1919).

3. Homer *Odyssey* 5.215–20; cf. 7.250–60.

4. Homer *Iliad* 14.323. All references are to the A. T. Murray translation (Cambridge, Mass.: Loeb Library, 1924).

5. *amphekalupsen* (Homer *Odyssey* 4.180; I am grateful to Keri Ames for pointing out to me the significance of this name).

6. Homer *Odyssey* 6.205–24.

7. Homer *Odyssey* 6.489–91.

8. Vyasa, *Mahabharata* (Poona: Bhandarkar Oriental Research Institute, 1933–69; critical ed.) 3, appendix 1.6.36–162; then 4.2.20 and 4.10. See also Wendy Doniger O'Flaherty, *Women, Androgynes, and Mythical Beasts* (Chicago: University of Chicago Press, 1981), p. 298.

9. Nick Allen argues for a general parallel between the Arjuna and Odysseus cycles, though he does not single out Calypso as a direct parallel to Urvashi, as I wish to do. See Nick Allen, "The Hero's Five Relationships: A Proto-Indo-European Story," in *Myth and Mythmaking: Continuous Evolution in Indian Tradition*, ed. Julia Leslie (Richmond, Surrey: Curzon Press, 1966), pp. 15–30.

10. Ovid, *Metamorphoses*, trans. Frank Justus Miller (Cambridge, Mass.: Loeb Library, 1977), 7.700–865.

11. This rather Cartesian tradition of mythology, denying the body to affirm the soul, stands in contrast to a dominant strain in Christian theology, which argues, as Caroline Walker Bynum has so brilliantly demonstrated (in *The Resurrection of the Body in Western Christianity, 200–1336* [New York: Columbia University Press, 1995]), that the body, too, is immortal. But I am limiting myself here to the mythology.

12. Jean Giraudoux, *Three Plays: Amphitryon, Intermezzo, Ondine*, trans. Roger Gellert (New York: Oxford University Press, 1967), p. 237.

13. Paracelsus, "A Book on Nymphs, Sylphs, Pygmies, and Salamanders, and on the Other Spirits," in *Four Treatises of Theophrastus von Hohenheim: Called Paracelsus*, trans. and intro. Henry E. Sigerist (Baltimore: Johns Hopkins University Press, 1990 [1914]).

14. S. Baring-Gould, *Curious Myths of the Middle Ages*, ed. Edward Hardy (New York: Oxford University Press, 1978), pp. 470–79.

15. Alexander H. Krappe, "Far Eastern Fox Lore," *California Folklore Quarterly* 3 (1944):138.

16. Otto Weininger, *Sex and Character*, cited by Marjorie Garber, *Vested Interests: Cross-Dressing and Cultural Anxiety* (New York and London: Routledge, 1992), p. 224.

17. Søren Kierkegaard, *Frygt og Baeven* (*Fear and Trembling*) in *Samlede Voerker*, vol. 5 (Copenhagen: Gyldendal, 1982), pp. 86–87; cited by Jacobsen in Per S. Jacobsen and Barbara Fass Leavy, *Ibsen's Forsaken Merman: Folklore in the Late Plays* (New York: New York University Press, 1988), p. 115.

18. Jacobsen and Leavy, *Ibsen's Forsaken Merman*, p. 18.

19. Gregory Nagy, "The Name of Apollo," in *Apollo: Origins and Influences* (Tucson: University of Arizona Press, 1994), p. 6.

20. Roberto Calasso, *The Marriage of Cadmus and Harmony* (New York: Alfred Knopf, 1993), p. 125.

21. Wendy Doniger, "Myths and Methods in the Dark," *Journal of Religion* 76:4 (October 1996):531–47.

22. Vyasa, *Mahabharata*, 3.52–54.

23. Robert A. Johnson, *Femininity Lost and Regained* (New York: Harper & Row, 1990), pp. 69–70.

24. Harsha, *Naishadiyacarita* (Bombay: Nirnaya Sagara Press, 1986), 6.95, 99, 105.

25. Valmiki, *Ramayana* (Baroda: Oriental Institute, 1960–75; critical ed.), 3.4.14.

26. Barbara Fass Leavy, *In Search of the Swan Maiden: A Narrative on Folklore and Gender* (New York: New York University Press, 1994), p. 277.

27. Barbara Fass, *La Belle Dame sans Merci and the Aesthetics of Romanticism* (Detroit: Wayne State University Press, 74), p. 35.

28. Angela Carter, "The Tiger's Bride," in *The Bloody Chamber and Other Stories* (London: Victor Gollancz, 1979; Harmondsworth: Penguin Books, 1981), p. 53.

29. This evocative phrase was suggested by Robert J. Lifton, personal communication, July 27, 1993.

30. This lovely phrase was coined by the singer Phyllis Curtin, in her response to an early variant of this essay, at Boston University Institute for Philosophy and Religion on April 12, 1995.

31. Thanks to Stephanie Nelson for this quote.

32. David Tracy, *On Naming the Present: Reflections on God, Hermeneutics, and Church* (Maryknoll, N.Y.: Orbis Books, 1994), p. 16.

33. Wendy Doniger O'Flaherty, *The Origins of Evil in Hindu Mythology* (Berkeley: University of California Press, 1976), chap. 7.

34. *Ibid.*, chap. 9.

35. Verrier Elwin, *Myths of Middle India* (London: Oxford University Press, 1949), p. 416.

36. *Ibid.*, p. 411.

37. *Ibid.*, p. 426.

38. W. H. Rivers, *The Todas* (London, 1906), p. 400.

39. Shakespeare *Hamlet* 1.2.12.

40. Wei-Yi Li, "On Becoming a Fish: Paradoxes of Immortality and Enlightenment in Chinese Literature," paper presented at the Einstein Forum conference on "Transformations of the Self," at Kibbutz Genosar on the Sea of Galilee, April 5–8, 1998.

41. Homer, *Homeric Hymn to Demeter*, trans. Hugh G. Evelyn-White (Cambridge, Mass.: Harvard University Press, 1914).

42. Giraudoux, *Amphitryon*, in *Three Plays*, p. 38.

43. Sir James George Frazer, *The Belief in Immortality*, 3 vols. (London: Macmillan, 1913)1:74–75, quoting A. C. Krujit, "De legenden der Poso-Alfoeren aangaande de erste menschen," in *Mededeelingen van wege het Nederlandsche Zendelinggenootschap*, xxxviii (1894), p. 340.

44. Hesiod tells the story twice, in the *Theogony* and the *Works and Days*. See Hesiod, *Theogony, Works and Days*, trans. Hugh G. Evelyn-White (Cambridge, Mass.: Loeb Library, 1914).

45. Hesiod, *Theogony*, pp. 453–506.

46. Claude Lévi-Strauss, *The Jealous Potter* (Chicago: University of Chicago Press, 1988), p. 71.

47. Carlo Ginzburg, *Ecstasies: Deciphering the Witches' Sabbath*, trans. Raymond Rosenthal (New York: Pantheon Books, 1991), p. 241, citing A. Szabo, "Der halbe Mensch und der Biblische Sündenfall," *Paideuma* 2 (1942–43): 95–100, and faulting him for comparing this story with the myth of Plato's symposium.

48. From Chiri Masashibo, *Chiri Masashibo Chosakshu* [Selected Works] (Tokyo: Kibonsha, 1973), 2:196. I am grateful to James Ketelaar for giving me this text, and translating it for me.

49. Homer, "Hymn to Demeter."

50. *Katha Upanishad, passim.*

51. Sir James George Frazer, *Taboo and the Perils of the Soul*, vol. 3, part 2 of *The Golden Bough* (New York: Macmillan, 1950), 1:70.

52. *Ibid.*, 1:74; P. Jos. Meier, *Mythe und Erzählungen der Küstenbewohner der Gazelle Halbinsel* (Berlin: Anthropos Bibliothek, 1909), 1:39.

53. Roheim, "The Garden of Eden," p. 20.

54. *Ibid.*, p. 21.

55. Malinowski, 1926, pp. 103–5.

56. Joel C. Kuipers, *Power and Performance: The Creation of Textual Authority in Weyewa Ritual Speech* (Philadelphia: University of Pennsylvania Press, 1990), p. 36.

57. Virgil *Aeneid* 6.719–43.

58. Lao-tzu *Tao te ching* 2; thanks to Stephanie Nelson.

59. Dylan Thomas, "Do Not Go Gentle into That Good Night" (1952); William Ernest Henley, "Invictus" (1888).

60. Salman Rushdie, *The Wizard of Oz* (London: British Film Institute, 1992), p. 57.

61. William Butler Yeats, "The Stolen Child," verses 2 and 4.

PART III

The Philosophy of Life and the Problem of Immortality

The Vague Hope of Immortality

JOHN LACHS

THE EASIEST WAY to understand the desire for immortality is from the standpoint of the isolated individual. Marco Polo went to China and lived on; why could the soul not seek its fulfillment and retain its integrity in alien worlds? If the quintessential *I* is a substance, as Descartes surmised, it could travel from one universe to the next, from here through purgatory to the place above, without losing its bearings. The worlds it would visit might seem strange at first, but such a universal spirit would soon feel comfortable anywhere.

The demand for immortality might also express our love of existence or our desire not to relinquish the satisfactions of communal life. Such desires betoken the social commitments of people, but they lead to insuperable problems for developing a conception of immortality. I will deal with these issues later.

The idea of self-sufficient individuals, on the other hand, is compatible with virtually any notion of the afterlife precisely because such persons are strangers in every world, floating as detached globules of intelligence on the surface of events. The problem here is that even if we manage to come up with some consistent notion of immortality, we have no sensible idea of the self on which to graft it; the idea of the isolated individual is incoherent.

So my argument is this. A sound conception of the self leaves us without any helpfully concrete notion of an afterlife, and any notion of immortality worth a second look presupposes an indefensible idea of who we are. I begin with this popular but wrongheaded account of the self.

I

A very large number of things and facts have no bearing on our lives. The age of the universe, the precise distance from my wife's skirt

127

to the outskirts of the Andromeda galaxy, and the intensity with which Tristan loved Isolde hold little significance for any of us. The existence of two or three people who play basketball better than I fails to disturb my equanimity.

Some matters should not be of concern to people, but they are. I wear glasses in an odd fashion, perched an inch above my ears. A few weeks ago, an acquaintance walked up to me and said wearing glasses in that way was stupid. The angle of their tilt annoyed him. I invited him to look the other way, where there might be sights to please. Leaving others alone is a virtue in desperate search of people to embody it.

Yet some elements in the alignment of the world are of vital significance to us in the prime of life and even when we prepare to die. Interestingly, these are not the usual concerns about future prospects and health, but solicitude for the people, even the objects, dear to us. The birdbath and cherry tree that shaped and shaded many a day in my young life matter to me even today. In gratitude, I wish them well; I want them to continue to exist, partly for their own sake because they were splendid, and partly so they may fill other young souls with peace and pleasure.

We feel the same way about people who share our lives. I want my wife, children, students, and friends to thrive after I die. In fact, it cheers me to think that they will, carrying a small part of me in their souls. I know very well that *I* will not in any significant sense *live* in them, yet that people vitally important to me will continue and do well matters profoundly.

In this and in many other respects, we differ from brutish tyrants. When Attila died, his wife and his servants were slain, so that they could serve him in the other world or at least not enjoy the benefits of this one. Attila's heirs are those who, having tested positive for HIV, seek unprotected sex with a multitude of partners. Angry over their fate, they want to take as many people with them as they can.

There has been a striking change in the sentiment of humans since Attila's day. Forcing healthy individuals to share a dead ruler's fate was then considered unobjectionable and perhaps even right. Today, by contrast, people who attempt to spread their misfortune by force or guile create revulsion in their neighbors and invite prosecution under the criminal code.

The matter is not one of enlightened self-interest. Wishing others well and aiding them may be the best strategy for a long and happy life. But when death is half a block away, plans for a long journey are beside the mark. For egoists, imminent death dissolves the restraints required for successful life and opens the door to whatever promotes immediate delight. If humans were expressions of a selfish gene, nearness of the end would make them sociopaths.

That this happens only on rare occasions shows how deeply we are entwined with our world. The view of humans as isolated, self-centered pools of aggression derives its plausibility from a narrow selection of examples. When Hobbes says, for example, that "the condition of man . . . is a condition of war of everyone against everyone,"[1] he is universalizing the occasional experiences of ordinary people and the state of mind of many a king and ruler. Careful observation of human life discredits such remarks; mothers tend not to wage war on their children and lovers sometimes protect each other at the cost of their own lives.

Human relations are not always cooperative, but nurturing activities are no more aberrations from our warlike stance than going to war is love by other means. If war is the paradigm of human activity, selfishness does not look foolish; but if we start from the tender support we offer those we love, narrow self-seeking seems to have no hold on our nature. At the very least, therefore, we must acknowledge a selfish and a social side to who we are.

But this still gives too much to the loner and the egoist. The war of "everyone against everyone" is not the struggle of one against the world or of individual against individual. War is a social act in which the combatants are ever in search of comrades and allies. Friends or fellow citizens feed and clothe the soldiers; those who risk their lives have children and lovers waiting for their return. Without cooperation, war would be impossible.

Collaboration, as any human activity, does not leave the soul untouched. The self expands to embrace the persons and objects close to it. The line between self and other melts when the other is a companion of many years, a well-loved dog, or one's familiar and comfortable home. The economy of the self expands, in this way, to include a portion of the world much larger than one's body and one's soul; it spreads from the center of the narrow self into the surrounding community, mixing its substance with whatever shares its interests or aids it.

This expansion of the self is not unique to humans. Dogs defend their territory and protect their owners loyally. With them, as with humans, gallant actions follow naturally, almost automatically, and not as the result of inferences or calculations. Assaulting the owner's child is no different from aggression against the dog; which of them was threatened cannot be gleaned from the fury of the counterattack.

Some people are so committed to others that they fear their own end less than the thought that those they love with all their hearts may die. This may explain why humans can reach a level of heroism in their defense of beloved others. If actions are reliable signs of commitments, we have reason to believe that some of them, when they face a forced choice, opt unhesitatingly for the welfare of others over their own. Mothers interpose themselves between their children and danger. Soldiers throw themselves on hand grenades to save the lives of their comrades. And, though I fight fiercely when anyone attacks me, that energy is insignificant compared to my rage at seeing someone hurt my children or my wife.

When the ego expands to encompass a multitude of things and persons, these initially external realities do not remain foreign objects; they are incorporated into the self and become constitutive of it. People who love what they do define themselves by their professions, treasuring the tools they use and the places where they work. Many humans live primarily in their relationships and view themselves as mothers, fathers, or friends rather than as individuals whose wants deserve first consideration. And we tend to think that referring to the country of our birth or the region where we grew up is adequate to explain what we value and who we are.

Seeing individuals as separate from one another and confined within their bodies provides, therefore, a distorted picture of the facts. On the contrary, persons overlap with one another in all sorts of ways, some of which create the tenderest relations while others serve as sources of deadly conflict. Under favorable circumstances, father and mother merge into each other and unite once again in the joint embrace of their child. But when rivals seek the same mate, incorporating it through the relations of constant attention and fierce desire, the overlap is unbearable and leads to strife.

With selves that overlap and criss-cross in a multitude of ways, it is not surprising that we take an intense interest in how we leave the world. In departing it, we leave large portions of ourselves behind. The persons and things that satisfy us do so not as alien forces; they are elements of who we are. Death is horrible, therefore, not because it threatens non-existence but because it cleaves the person and imposes an inevitable parting. When we close our eyes for the last time, we are separated from a world we love, that is, from our very selves; the severed person bleeds, as what gave us such delight remains behind and the impulse to caress it is no more. We are not self-centered, independent globules of consciousness.

II

The desire not to die may also be a natural outcome of our love of life. So many of the things we do delight us that we never want to stop; if we can run and laugh and eat and love well, why should the fun not go on for century after glorious century? We are reluctant to close down the activities of a prosperous life because they are going so well, and of a life of suffering and loss because we might soon turn it around. In either case, whenever the end seems imminent, we think that just a little more time might get us ready to go.

Yet what would it be like to live on without a natural conclusion? The Sibyl was granted endless life without eternal youth; such an existence of wheezing decline and chronic pain over thousands of years cannot be attractive to anyone. Since the body wears out, causing misery, any life worth continuing has to be in a realm free from decay. There we may enjoy the peace of blessedness, singing the praises of the Lord and perhaps seeing God face-to-face. In that shining world, time and the losses it exacts are forgotten and we can rejoice in the glory of what we do and who we are.

But what can we do and who exactly are we in that world? The only positive ideas we can entertain about this realm are those we steal from life here; we speak of peace and singing and seeing someone face-to-face. The humble origin of such words as "shine" and "rejoicing" reminds us that their spiritual function derives from what the animal in us appreciates. The rest of the ideas that give content to the notion of heaven relate to our existence by negation. That the afterlife is free from the ravages of time, that neither loss nor disappointment can touch us there amount only to reassuring denials that that world is not as flawed as this.

The origin of the constituent ideas of heaven and the negativity of much of our conception of it are nevertheless inadequate to strip it

of legitimacy. There may well be realities we can approach only nega-
tively or by analogy. Yet a careful look at the concept calls attention to
what in our fervent desire for blessedness we may forget: that what
we hope for is baffling or hopelessly vague.

If I were an individual of the sort Hobbes, let alone Descartes,
imagined, heaven would be easy to define. It would be life that is the
opposite of "nasty, brutish, and short"—let us say pleasant, perhaps
even elegant, humane, and very long. As a single agent pursuing a private good, I could feel at home in any cozy corner. So long as I remained free and secure and in possession of such instruments of pleasure as the good will of God, I would need nothing; the fortunes of
others would sound like tales from a distant planet.

But we are not insular individuals whose direct relation to God
suffices for satisfaction. Heaven would be like a concentration camp
if entering it separated us from those we love. We are complex social
beings who cannot flourish apart from companions and family. We incorporate them into our larger selves, just as they find room for us in
their souls. Such inclusion is not an occasional or accidental nicety; it
constitutes the fabric of our being. We are parts of each other, and the
parts others constitute account for the bulk of each of us.

I have already spoken of the indissoluble bonds between the self
and its community. William James speaks of this remarkable unity in
terms of the expansion of the boundaries of the self. G. H. Mead and
others think there could be no self and hence no broadening of its horizons without the environment, the impetus, and the materials the
world of others provides. In either case, satisfaction of the individual is
impossible without the concurrent well-being of significant portions of
the community. Heaven must, therefore, be a friendly and a social
place, where the good fortune of all is the condition of the delight of
anyone.

III

So far so good for our idea of heaven. For our moral convictions
confirm that this conception of an afterlife is on the right track. People
generally agree that it is wrong to be indifferent to the fate of others
and repugnant to take pleasure in their distress. So it should be unacceptable for those who enjoy eternal bliss to delight in invidious com-
parisons between their good fortune and the sad fate of those whose

pleas for blessedness are denied. The morally right conception of the afterlife depicts heaven as the fulfillment of our social impulses, achieving at last the perfect coincidence of the good of the individual with the interests of the community.

The desire for such a harmony of people with their neighbors reveals the struggles of which we wish to be relieved. Yet it is in these and other struggles that we have our lives, and that is the source of the trouble for our idea of heaven. In the natural course of events, fulfillments flow from efforts and bring them to a smiling end. We can distinguish the two, but we cannot separate them. Effort without result is frustrating and vain; pleasure with no need for exertion is curiously hollow. Only the two together satisfy, the one as price and preparation, the other as conclusion and reward. We might think of them as two parts of a natural human act in which, in the absence of endeavor, even pleasure does not please.

Admittedly, nothing seems easier than to detach our moments of delight from the events that generate them and to think of benefits without their costs. Adolescent males notoriously dream of being objects of the attention of exquisite women showering pleasures on their grateful parts. They think of themselves as quivering sensoria absorbing gratification without having to do anything to earn or to sustain it. A ready receptivity, they believe, is all we need to lead the good life.

This, however, is the stuff of daydreams. Two considerations show that it is fantasy. The adolescent mind, anxious for quick release, sees all labor and deferral as pain. It needs much attentive experience to carry it from chugging beer to the discriminating pleasures of wine tasting. The revelation that the pleasures of eating come to more than gulping food and that hasty orgasms never do justice to love dawns on it slowly. Perhaps only later in life does the role of process in pleasure become clear. Then we realize that the bulk of our delight in eating resides in what might be seen as grinding labor, but what in the performance is experienced with a measure of satisfaction—in biting, tearing, chewing, and swallowing. We also learn that much of the pleasure of love is in foreplay, in the fevered movement of bodies and in the play of building to, yet resisting, consummation.

The element of the human condition to which these comments point is not that our satisfactions are bought with suffering. If we were speaking merely of a causal connection, we could always try to substitute alternative conditions to generate what we want; we could hope to eliminate the pains and burdens of life by the comforts of technology.

But the relationship is much more intimate. We can enjoy only or primarily what is laborious and requires effort. Since pure sensation and unadulterated pleasure are past our ken, we feel little delight without the process of working for it. God's malediction that "in the sweat of thy face shalt thou eat bread" is even more horrendous than it must have sounded to Adam and to Eve; it decrees not only that we must pay for everything we get, but also that we cannot take joy in anything unsaturated by the agony of our labor.

We are, in brief, condemned to pain and cursed in our pleasures. The theology of this twilight condition has been only partially explored. We know that Adam's sin erased the possibility of a life of easy harmony. But the punishment for disobedience is typically supposed to take the form only of pain. Little attention has been paid to the wrenching adjustment God's curse wrought in our nature, making our pleasures dependent on our pains and turning our lives into a sad and glorious victory-in-defeat. The fall rendered us masochists not in our intentions but in our activities and enjoyments, in the innermost recesses of our nature.

The way pleasure occurs constitutes the second reason for the inseparability of satisfaction from exertion. When things go well, fulfillment appears to be effortless or automatic. The ease with which it comes may lull us into believing that when we enjoy pleasure, we *do* nothing. This impression is reinforced by the sense of passivity that accompanies some sensory indulgences. A backscratch or a hot shower generates delights that seem to involve no activities on our parts. All we need to do is let another's fingers walk or the hot water run, and simply be present for the sensory consequences.

This, however, is an incomplete picture of what actually takes place. The feeling of passivity supervenes upon the humming activity of the sensory and the nervous systems. But more, the enjoyment has to be varied and sustained. Visions of beauty lapse unless they are renewed again and again by keeping the head stable and refocusing the eyes. No satisfaction is lasting without exercising sufficient control over circumstances to maintain the feeling. Even in the shower, the passivity we experience is framed in activities of the sort required for standing up instead of collapsing on the floor, remaining erect under the stream of water rather than leaning until one falls out of the tub, and moving from time to time to let the water hit different parts of the body.

In truth, we do not know how to be passive, no matter how much we try. And the point is that we have to *try*, meaning that we have to expend energy to reach the stage where exertion is not needed. Yet, or just because of this, we never actually get there: attaining the level of passive enjoyments or costless benefits is impossible. This, again, is the human condition of being unable to enjoy anything to whose existence or nature we make no contribution. Whether we read this in theological terms as due to the fall of Adam or in naturalistic ones as the fate of animals struggling in an adverse environment, the fact that, for us at least, enjoyment without labor is inconceivable remains a structuring feature of our lives.

IV

What, then, of our notion of an afterlife? I exclude from consideration ideas according to which death is followed by absorption in the life force or in the peace of nothingness. However reassuringly such views are expressed, they invariably imply personal extinction. I am interested in what content we can give the hope that our individuality will not be erased without a trace. Sitting in a delightfully seedy McAnn's bar in New York one day, I heard a distinguished philosopher say, "If heaven has no McAnn's, I'm not interested." Though the sentiment is easy to appreciate, an afterlife no different or no better than existence today cannot serve as a motivating ideal. A life worse than this, moreover, is not an object of hope. We can of course always conceive a world better in some particular: one, for example, in which I have hair, you more money, or all of us fewer terrible diseases. But such worlds constitute objectives of reasonable striving; to achieve them, we need knowledge and luck rather than life everlasting.

That leaves a life that is problem-free and consists of an unbroken string of satisfactions. Such a heavenly existence would have to be social, but without the usual costs of communal life, that is, without friction, anxiety, destructive competition, conflicting interests, and debilitating hatreds. We simply have no idea what such an existence would be like. On the personal level, we cannot even think of enjoying what we did not labor to attain or to sustain. On the social side, we cannot imagine human interaction free of conflict and struggle.

Marx thought that such harmonious social life would become possible after the socialist revolution. But when it came time for him to say what it might consist of, he had nothing more positive to offer than that it would allow us to fish in the morning, hunt in the afternoon, and do philosophy in the evening. If these were its hallmarks, heaven on earth would make for a painfully boring, deeply dissatisfying world. Would we want to go angling if the fish jumped in the boat when we embarked? Would we enjoy hunting if the quarry rushed up to us, died on the spot, and promptly turned itself into a savory dish? Could we get anything out of philosophy without criticism and disagreement? A world of diversified but easy activities is particularly tedious precisely because it lacks the problems that give a keen edge to life. The bulk of human togetherness is focused on solving or at least on coping with problems, not on flaccid enjoyments. Without shared difficulties, the meaning and the small victories of existence quickly dissipate.

Just as we cannot embrace the joys of private life without becoming heirs to labor, so we cannot feed on the pleasures of community apart from the troubles social life resolves, and causes. The very structure of human caring is determined by the problems we face: our love for children and aging parents is saturated with concern for their well-being. We worry about them, fight to protect them, and work with them to overcome the obstacles in their way. Love unburdened by the predicaments of life is a single note tediously sustained, not a symphony. Good music, as good living, requires variety and enough discord to struggle with and to subdue in a broader harmony.

Our finite, ambiguous state affects not only individual activities and social life, but also the architecture of our selves. We are what our desires, struggles, and satisfactions make us. Much as we hope for the costless delights of heaven, we also seek the interesting—that means, the problematic—in life, and look for challenges to test our powers. We are made for this twilight world, and nothing shows the ambivalence of our condition more clearly than that we both love this life and wish to escape to something better.

I conclude that, given a proper understanding of the nature of selves, we have no specific, clear, and viable idea of a heavenly afterlife. This does not mean that we fail to survive the dissolution of our bodies or that there is no better world to which death opens the door. Since we lack adequate information, it is wise to withhold judgment on such issues, though the want of positive evidence should concern those who hope for eternal life. But even if there is an afterlife, we are not in a position to determine, or even to imagine, its nature.

To be sure, we can refer to it from a distance by external designators, just as we can speak of the millionth prime number by reference to the sequence of our systematic search, even though we do not know which number it is. But, alas, our idea of heaven is even vaguer than our current notion of the millionth prime number. For we know at least that the millionth prime number is a number, and we know precisely how we can find out which number it is. When we speak of costless pleasures and unproblematic social lives, by contrast, we literally do not know what we are saying. Joy and labor are indissolubly connected in this world, and if there are "pleasures" not surrounded by problems and supported by exertions, they are nothing like the delights we experience and know. We cannot grasp the nature of such satisfactions, and it is not even clear what right we have to refer to them by that honored name.

Aside from forming a concrete idea of heaven, supporters of the afterlife face an unanswered question concerning our identity there. Human self-identity is a function of experiences undergone and problems overcome. We are styles of operating in the world, built up over years of dealing with the contingencies of life. How could I be anyone in particular if I consisted of the same unproblematic joys as my neighbors? And how could I be the same person in heaven as I am here if my labored life becomes, past death, an ethereal song?

I cannot say that my two selves are united as are hope and its realization, because without a clear idea of heaven I cannot form meaningful hopes relating to it. And even if the later self knew the struggles of the earlier, it would have no basis for viewing them as its own. More likely, it would regard them as the butterfly does the travail of the distant worm that must die before the birth of wings and flight. So the beings that may succeed us would not remember us at all, and if they did, they would look upon our strivings and our joys as the experiences of aliens, rather than as the bumbling indiscretions of their childhoods.

Might it then be that the hope for immortality is a vague, ill-thought-out wish? When Shelley speaks of "the desire of the moth for the star," he has in mind a yearning both for what is difficult to reach and for what cannot be clearly grasped. Such longings are not uncommon among human beings; they often take the form of wanting something whose nature or consequences are inadequately explored.

King Midas came to grief because he wished for everything he touched to turn to gold, and Icarus plunged from the sky because he overlooked that the sun melts wax. Wanting to have all the money in the world or to have sex with everyone in the 82nd Airborne might sound like legitimate desires, but they engage the attention only of people who do not fully understand what is involved.

I suspect something like that is the case with the desire for immortality. A heavenly afterlife sounds like a good idea, so long as we do not examine it enough to realize that there is not much of a concrete idea there at all. The quest for endless life and limitless delight blinds us to the cognitive shortfall at the heart of our notion of immortality. Descartes was right when he pointed out that the human will, and hence human wants, are infinite but the intellect is finite. And he knew that the resulting pursuit of infinity gets us in trouble.[2]

Our tendency to break down barriers and to surmount all obstacles makes the magnitude of the trouble difficult to assess. The desire for immortality of the sort I have discussed is a transcendent or a religious version of our current social and scientific drive to overcome all the difficulties standing in the way of human fulfillment. The failed Marxist experiment in resocializing us is now supplanted by the hope for a wholesale genetic re-engineering of our natures. We think we can defeat aging, eliminate disease, and turn each of us into an exemplary specimen of our kind. Scientists tell us that nothing can stop us from converting this small planet into heaven but failure of resolve.

The cost of such grand but foolish drives is the loss of our souls. We are finite creatures with limited potential for satisfaction. Like cats, we love enclosed spaces and terminal movements; nothing pleases as much as a good beginning, a little progress along the way, and a cozy conclusion. The open-ended is a wound in the ordered world. Everything we deal with—sneezes and suppers and sentences—comes in small units, and we view the unfinished as gapingly incomplete. The infinite leaves us hungering for closure and sadly forgetful that everything is more precious when in short supply.

Why, then, would someone seek the infinite and want everlasting life? Only because intelligence has not extended its dominion over the heart. That we never perish and upon dying face a better life is an understandable hope of hard-pressed animals. That "we" in some sense are "immortal" may even be a proper object of faith. But it is a mistake to count on personal survival of death, and a pernicious error to think we need it to redeem this life. So long as we do the Lord's work and do not ask the Lord to do ours, we can make this world good enough for us. And when we die, it should be adequate consolation that we lived well and that our loved ones stay behind.

NOTES

1. Thomas Hobbes *Leviathan* chap. 14.
2. See Rene Descartes *Meditations on First Philosophy* 4.

"This Tablet, Which Itself Will Quickly Perish"

AARON V. GARRETT

I. INTRODUCTION

My essay is a comparison of the thoughts of John Locke and Benedict Spinoza on eternity and immortality. I hope that this comparison will tell us something valuable about the odd interrelation between eternity and immortality, and about their connection with other concepts such as morality and personhood. For both philosophers, a satisfactory account of how these concepts are interrelated must rest on an answer to a further question: Are we ultimately mortal beings desiring immortality or beings whose eternity is somehow distinct from any such strivings (as well as from any finite considerations of the world)? I will develop this issue first, and then show in turn how it impacts other considerations. It is an issue which Spinoza and Locke have treated in ways that, if neither eternal nor immortal, are edifying both for their thoughtfulness and their endurance.

II. LOCKE'S EPITAPH

John Locke's epitaph, which he wrote himself, reads:

Near this place lies John Locke. If you wonder what kind of man he was, the answer is that he was one contented with his modest lot. A scholar by training, he devoted his studies wholly to the pursuit of truth. Such you may learn of his writings, which will also tell you whatever else there is to be said about him more faithfully than the dubious elegies of an epitaph. His virtues, if he had any, were too slight to serve either to his own credit or as an example to you. Let his vices be interred with him. An example of virtue you have already in the Gospels; an example of vice is something one could wish did not exist; an example of mortality (and may you learn from it) you have assuredly here and everywhere. That he was born on August 29, 1632, and died on October 28, 1704, this tablet, which itself will quickly perish, is a record.[1]

This epitaph points to a central dichotomy. That which is expressed in Locke's writings, insofar as it is rational, is one sort of testament—a testament more faithful "than the dubious elegies of an epitaph." And clearly Locke thought that once he had died his writings would be the primary source both of his continuing posthumous value in this world and of what useful things others may learn of him. This is doubtless correct. We know Locke via his *Essay*, his *Second Treatise*, and a host of other writings. But Locke's fate, the John Locke who "was born on August 29, 1632, and died on October 28, 1704," is quite another thing. His writings may or may not be eternal, but any immortality that he himself might have will be between Locke and his Savior (as the crumbling tablet reminds us). And Locke's virtues and vices, which undergird his salvation, are only distinguished insofar as they are Locke's—and only of interest for Locke and perhaps his friends.

The difference that Locke points to appears to be a distinction between the thoughts I have had, and what I have written that can be accessed by future generations, and those things which concern my person—my moral virtues and vices. The former go on irrespective of my final destination (at least until the Day of Judgment); the latter only matter in relation to it (for Locke). And the two are likely separate; otherwise the salvation of the ignorant would be questionable. Thus in some sense my moral personality is separate from my everlasting intellectual accomplishment, and perhaps the latter is not *me* in as strong a sense as the former.

This distinction is related to the distinction between eternity and immortality. It seems fairly obvious that there is a difference between immortality and eternity. This difference is made apparent by a phrase used by John Locke's friend and theological fellow traveler, the Dutch theologian Phillip von Limborch. In his *System of Theology*, von Limborch remarked that Christ triumphs over the "eternity of death."[2] Now one can talk about the "eternity of death" (if slightly confusingly), but one certainly can't speak coherently about "the immortality of death." A similar passage from Locke also makes the dichotomy apparent: "shall give you this new and higher principle of a Spiritual life, i.e. of immortality *for him hath god the father sealed* which sealeing was when the spirit discended on him at his baptisme and he was declared the son of god, i.e., heir of eternal life (Mat III.16.17)."[3]

Immortality is about transcending, moving past, moving beyond, being redeemed as against death. Thus immortality is the "new and higher principle of a Spiritual life." Eternity is entirely independent of death—to the point that one can coherently speak of the "eternity of death" or contrast eternal punishment and immortality. Eternity may be defined in terms of time, or not, as the case may be. We can speak of the eternal present, of eternity as opposed to sempiternity, or the eternity of being. But the crucial distinction I would like to draw is a consequence of the relatively wide extension of eternity and the relatively narrow one of immortality. If we are eternal, that part of us which is eternal will not die and never would die—it has nothing to do with death. If we are immortal our immortality seems far more closely enmeshed with death. And only those beings we could imagine as dying, or at least ceasing to exist in some way that we consider analogous to death, could properly become immortal. The eternity of something, or an eternal something for that matter, would have little to do with this. My writings could be eternal or immortal, depending on whether they are expressions of eternal truths or perishable products transmitted from mind to mind by perishable beings who resemble them. But me, you, this tablet, my vices and virtues, and what they mean to me seem very mortal, and any way that they transcend mortality would appear to have much more to do with immortality than with eternity.

The very opposite of the death-soaked "immortalism" expressed on Locke's tablet, where the boundary between life and death means so much to us, is expressed in Benedict Spinoza's famous dictum "The free man thinks least of all about death, and his wisdom is not one of death, but rather is a meditation on life."[4] Spinoza was Locke's exact contemporary by birth (b. 1632) if not by death (Spinoza d. 1677, Locke d. 1704). There are numerous similarities between their philosophies that have drawn some to argue for the influence of Spinoza on Locke (as Spinoza's writings were available long before Locke's). They are often considered to be the two central "fathers of liberalism." They were also two of the most famous advocates of toleration in the

seventeenth century. They were perhaps the two most important figures of the late seventeenth century in the development of eighteenth-
century psychology and theories of the passions.

But on this issue, on the respective centrality of eternity and immortality to their philosophies, they could not be more irremediably
and instructively different. Spinoza emphasizes eternity and criticizes
the relevance of immortality. Locke emphasizes immortality and has
little place for the kind of eternity that Spinoza centralizes. Each option results in contrasting and telling problems. And although each describes morals as a naturally deducible system given what we know
about human nature and human desires, the centralizing of eternity or
immortality drastically changes its import. Put simply, from the perspective of Spinoza's eternity, morals are hardly discernible, whereas
for Locke they are a fundamental basis of the grant of immortality. But
first on to eternity.

III. SPINOZA ON ETERNITY AND IMMORTALITY

Spinoza's *Ethics* attempts to explain immortality by reducing it to
eternity. Spinoza defines eternity thus: "By eternity I understand existence itself, insofar as it is conceived to follow necessarily and solely
from the definition of a/the eternal thing."[5] Spinoza goes on to expli-
cate this passage by emphasizing that eternity cannot be explained via
any sort of duration. The main features of this definition for my essay
are: 1) Eternity is dependent not on us, or anything subjective, but
rather on that which is eternal as such; 2) Eternity is independent of
time, or beginnings and ends of any sort.

Any sort of eternity our minds might have is ultimately to be understood in relation to the eternal as such—God or Nature. Our minds
are eternal insofar as they are a part of the eternal and infinite intellect
of God, but the consequences of this fact for religion and immortality
are not quite so simple.

In the second to last proposition of the *Ethics*, Spinoza makes the
following rather surprising claim, "Even if we did not know that our
mind is eternal, we would still regard Morality and Religion as of the
first importance."[6] Our knowledge, or non-knowledge, of the eternity
of our minds has no direct impact on morality and religion, on our behavior towards others, on the communities we associate with, and so

forth. Knowledge of God, and our relation to him via natural reason, may be an essential *precondition* of morality and religion, but the truths of religion and morality are fully demonstrable without the additional knowledge of the eternity of our minds. Thus eternity and morality have little bearing on one another.

Spinoza develops this point by noting that most who read scripture, in particular the multitude, believe that divine law is something which takes away our freedom and curbs human desire. By binding themselves to this law, and giving up their freedom, they hope to get a reward—or to avoid a horrible punishment. This vision of religion is not just that of the multitude, and of numerous interpreters of scripture, but also of Hobbes and philosophers who view religion as a necessary control on the multitude via their hopes and fears.

Spinoza remarks:

> These opinions seem no less absurd to me than if someone, because he does not believe he can nourish his body with good food to eternity, should prefer to fill himself with poisons and other deadly things, or because he sees that the Mind is not eternal, or immortal, should prefer to be mindless, and to live without reason. These [common beliefs] are so absurd they are hardly worth mentioning.[7]

Thus, that which Spinoza sees as true morality and true religion must be rational for the human mind irrespective of its eternity. But what does Spinoza mean by this? Whatever morality and religion do for us, and in whatever way they ultimately contribute to our knowledge of the eternity of our mind, they do so in and through themselves without the promise of a goal external to them.

In claiming this, Spinoza explicitly identifies eternity and immortality. This is one of the very few times, and the only prominent one, where he uses the word "immortality" in the *Ethics*. We know from his *Cogitata Metaphysica* that Spinoza thought immortality distinct from eternity. There he discusses eternity, immortality, and mortality, in relation to creation and the human soul.

Spinoza argues that God is eternal, and by this he means that God's essence and existence are God himself, that God is absolutely necessary, and that duration (past, present, or future), however endless, cannot be applied to him. As a consequence, all of God's decrees and laws are also eternal insofar as they arise from the necessity of his essence. But this does not mean that *creatures* are eternal, or that God can communicate his eternity to creatures, or that the Son of God is a creature. So Spinoza uses the language of immortality, as opposed to eternity, to discuss the sort of existence creatures may be said to have beyond this particular finite life.

Spinoza begins *Cogitata Metaphysica* XII, "Of the human mind," by distinguishing between theological and natural knowledge, and asserting that "theological knowledge is altogether other than, or completely different in kind from natural knowledge." As such the philosopher is interested only in fixed and settled laws, and does "not ask, when we speak of the soul, what God can do, but only what follows from the laws of nature." Following this strict limiting of his claims *to* natural reason, Spinoza immediately confronts the problem of treating immortality *within* natural reason. For, if the soul is created, then it can be destroyed, since "he who has the power of creating a thing also has the power of destroying it." But substances cannot be destroyed, whether extended substance as such, or thinking substance, or God— although the particular structure of a body can.

From these considerations Spinoza concludes, "it follows clearly from the laws of nature that the soul is immortal" and "that God's immutable will concerning the duration of souls has been manifested to men not only by revelation, but by the natural light." Yet this claim seems odd. Either one must prove something stronger than the mere "duration of souls" from the existence of substance, or something weaker, that we have infinite duration. This does not follow from likeness to substance, however, as substance is eternal and not of endless duration. This latter point is amplified by a further tangle. If, as just noted, the "structure of the body" can be destroyed even if corporeal substance is eternal, then why not the structure of the soul even if thinking substance too is eternal? And if the structure of the soul is destroyed, what sort of individual is left?

Thus we have an additional problem of immortality. We can say *in abstractu* that the soul is *eternal*. But *if* we argue that the soul is *immortal*, insofar as this particular soul continues in its existence, this cannot just be a consequence of the eternity of substance. Thus the relation that this finite being has to death has nothing to do with the relation between substance and the fixed laws of nature.

This is related to the most well-known problem of Book V of the *Ethics*: that Spinoza discusses the eternity of the mind at great length, but not the correspondent eternity of the body. In Spinoza's theory of how bodies are individuated, a given body has a specific ratio of motion and rest, and thus its parts have a certain consistent structural relation to each other, even if the particular parts are ever changing. For example, my skin changes every seven years but maintains a consistent ratio of motion and rest to my changing blood supply and my changing kidneys. If the particular structure is destroyed it seems to follow that the body is also destroyed, and it is hard to see what it means for it to continue. The matter may continue, but not the structure, and the matter according to Spinoza does not a body make.

The case of the mind is analogous. *My mind* as a whole *is not eternal* for Spinoza. The imagination, senses, and memory are not eternal. But my *intellect*—the active rational component of my mind—is. It considers things as if under a species of eternity. It views things independent of their enduring existence, and as such has no content that is in any way tied to particular existence, unlike my imagination and body. But what, then, holds together and individuates my mind?

This is a real problem. Remember that Spinoza's eternity of the mind has nothing to do with mortality, since mortality does not view things as if they are eternal. Therefore the only possible strategy Spinoza can have for dealing with immortality is to replace it with eternity and to ignore the dross of mortal existence. Thus, Spinoza equates immortality and eternity in the *Ethics*, claiming that eternity has successfully taken the place of immortality. The dross of mortal existence, however, is more of a problem than Spinoza admits. Morals for Spinoza primarily involve relations between limited finite beings. They assume my individual desires which express themselves through thought and extension, which have little to do with the eternal in me. Little which I recognize as truly *me*—my vicious and virtuous acts, my passions and sentiments about others—are recognizable in the eternal at all. In the deepest sense, they are not me.

So, what is death for Spinoza, given the choice of eternity over immortality? It could be a birth into freedom and awakeness—as for Plotinus. For when I die, if that part of me which was most rational ceased to have any concern with that part of me which worried about death, I would be reborn as a free man. The quote with which I introduced Spinoza seems to imply this: "a free man thinks of nothing less than of death, and his wisdom is a meditation on life, not on death";[8] as well as: "if men were born free, they would form no concept of good &

evil so long as they remained free." But to say that this part of us is what is eternal and free is really idle speculation about death, and thus terribly unfree. It is looking at such freedom as if we would never enter again another state which would cloud and muddle this freedom. It is as if freedom is an *immortal* passage to a better state, and of course this is far beyond anything we can know rationally. All we can know rationally is that the part of us which is eternal is the part of us which is rational; not that it has anything to do with immortality. And to think about it, as opposed to reveling in the eternity of reason, goes against the dictum with which we began our discussion of Spinoza:

> These opinions seem no less absurd to me than if someone, because he does not believe he can nourish his body with good food to eternity, should prefer to fill himself with poisons and other deadly things, or because he sees that the Mind is not eternal, or immortal, should prefer to be mindless, and to live without reason. These [common beliefs] are so absurd they are hardly worth mentioning.[9]

In worrying and idly speculating about my duration I am preferring mindlessness to the activities of reason. I could at that very moment be liberating the eternity in the moment through reason, turning mere immortality into eternity, and becoming free irrespective of the when or where.

What does it mean that we know ourselves to be eternal? We recognize a feature of our minds (and perhaps our bodies) as eternal, but this feature has nothing to do with our moral conduct. Morality is neither a necessary nor a sufficient condition of eternity, as the man born free would be beyond good and evil and thus beyond morality. But our moral self-understanding as a finite being related to other finite beings in a vast nexus is temporal and transitory and has nothing of those features of my mind which are eternal.

How do I know that I am eternal? I know *in abstractu*, insofar as it follows from the rational way in which I understand Nature—the metaphysical structure of the world—and the place of my mind in it. And this recognition of my eternity is something powerful, a kind of self-recognition where that part of my intellect which is eternal recognizes itself, however abstractly, through its own intellectual activity. This self-recognition is also the joyous recognition that part of my mind is God's love of God's self, and the love of God I have is eternal.[10] This love is a very special sort of cognition, which arises from and recognizes those eternal aspects of our minds insofar as we know ourselves to be in and through God.

However moving such a picture is, I ought not think that it has anything to do—alas—with the me I normally recognize, the me who feels obliged to others, who behaves in this or that manner. That falls by the wayside. It is a purified metaphysical me; all finite baggage and property have been thrown overboard. This morality, deducible by reason, is a feature of a finite me which at its best is something entirely else. This is certainly not the case for Locke.

IV. LOCKE ON IMMORTALITY

Unlike Spinoza, immortality as such is central to Locke's philosophy. One might say, with little exaggeration, that immortality and death are *the* central issues of Christianity for Locke beyond the minimal creed offered in the *Reasonableness of Christianity*. Adam's transgression brought death into the world, and Jesus' sacrifice brought the possibility of immortality. The "wages of sin" are to be understood literally as death. Hell is death; and paradise, at least in part, eternal life. The dichotomy between life and death, and the promise of immortality, suffuses Locke's notion of a bare-bones Christianity.

In the *Essay* Locke makes strong distinctions between philosophy and theology. He developed his theory of personal identity in large part to avoid having to reduce one's identity to a soul (or a body). In the *First Treatise* he attacked Filmer for making unwarranted assumptions about the meaning of original sin within the context of politics. The separation of theology from politics, and philosophy, is crucial to his understanding of toleration and the role of the state. Like Spinoza, Locke is a paradigmatic thinker of these separations.

And, like Spinoza, Locke saw the truths of morals to be derivable via natural reason. For Locke this was a historical fact. Much that could be found in the New Testament had its precursors in statements of the ancient Greeks and Romans. What differentiated Jesus' presentation of these moral truths from the many thinkers of the past is not their content, but rather their completeness with no remainder.[11] All of the ancient moral doctrines have something wrong with them. Epicurus, for example, has sayings consistent with the New Testament, but he also made statements that were, well, Epicurean in the baser sense. The same could be said of Socrates and Plato.

Thus, although these moral truths are deducible by more or less perfect reasoners, and thus are evidence of the deducibility of morals via natural reason, they are also usually accompanied by mistakes or extensions beyond the essential core of moral philosophy. Furthermore they were often limited in time and place, and to a select group of people. Jesus presented a complete, universal, accessible, and rational morality. That, according to Locke, is—like Jesus' miracles—a sign of his divinity.

Spinoza would assent to some of this, although he would take strong exception to the claim that the perfection of a moral doctrine is a sign of divinity. Locke, even more than Spinoza, saw the importance of this core moral doctrine in the salvation of the ignorant and poor—thus liberating morality and religion from interpretive Pharisees. But none of this takes away from the rationality of the doctrine. In fact, it shows that in the form of Jesus' teaching it has a fully rational, complete, and integrated presentation.

For Locke there is another feature of such a complete, universal, accessible, and rational moral doctrine which certainly Spinoza does not accept. This feature makes the above point somewhat tenuous. It is that this moral doctrine should be understood as a law that obliges, and by which one is judged, because, according to Locke, Jesus "has given us an unquestionable assurance and pledge of it in his own resurrection and ascension into heaven." This is what ultimately distinguishes the natural morality of the Greeks and Romans from Christianity. As to virtue:

> That she is the perfection and excellency of our nature; that she is herself a reward, and will recommend our name to future ages, is not all that can now be said of her. It is not strange that the learned heathens satisfied not many with airy commendations. It has another relish and efficacy to persuade men, that if they live well they will be happy hereafter. . . . The view of heaven and hell will cast a flight upon the short pleasures and pains of this present state, and give attractions and encouragements to virtue. . . . Upon this foundation, and upon this only, morality stands firm and may defy all competition.[12]

Heathen rational morality may promote virtue, but it lacks both a Lawgiver and visceral consequences for the satisfaction or nonsatisfaction of the law. Thus it will only be followed by an elite few, and these only within this life. As there is no reward but the virtues of the actions themselves, and whatever health of body and mind follow from them, countless will pay lip service to morals without any actual virtue. But Jesus, in addition to presenting the perfect natural morality, has also appended to it the possibility of immortality, and thus attached to it cosmic and, well, eternal consequences. Thus appending immortality to morality allows all to know the joys of morality, and gives us the possibility of immortal life.

This is immortality we are dealing with, not eternity. It is precisely the contrast between our present state and our future state that Locke emphasizes as the basis for our desire to satisfy the law. What we do within the present state, morally, has great consequences for our future state. Therefore immortality is attached to, but barely outside the ken of, natural morality and natural reason.

This "barely outside" is the problem, when it comes to immortality. The difficulty for Locke is fairly obvious, but serious. If moral laws hold, irrespective of any grant of immortality, but just as a consequence of natural reason, then immortality and future expectation become unimportant. And Jesus is merely a teacher, as for Spinoza. But if an immortal guarantee is the essential feature of the law, then the naturally deducible moral system is dependent on something supernatural—for what could be more supernatural than immortality?

Throughout the *Reasonableness of Christianity* and the *Paraphrases* of Paul's Epistles Locke dances around this problem, weakly committing himself in both directions.[13] It makes practical sense not to commit himself strongly, as each side points to "error." Stillingfleet and Leibniz thought Locke possibly a materialist; others thought Locke's Christianity far too rational, and thought it did away with the divinity of Christ entirely. These two points were not mutually exclusive. They combined to form the accepted picture of the heresy of all heresies: Socinianism. What is interesting for Locke, as opposed to the picture painted of Locke by his critics, is that they have an uneasy and perhaps even a contradictory relation in his philosophy. On the one hand Locke affirms the power of divine volition, and the fact that a law must be given by an external Lawgiver (very unlike Spinoza's immanent decrees) in order to obligate and to need satisfaction.[14] And of course it arises from Locke's reading of Jesus' words, and interpreting Paul through them. Locke's rationalism in morals is a consequence of his general belief in the reasonableness of Christianity, and in the human role in discovering it. It appears possible for a perfect intellect to discover this rationally deducible morality, without obligations and sanctions attached. But it is not possible for any of us, and therefore the problem of immortality as reward sits in between.

Thus, when we bundle immortality with natural reason, and particularly natural morality, things become difficult. A very good example of this for Locke is his discussion of personal identity,[15] which is tied up in its genesis with Locke's struggles with the problems of the natural immortality of the soul. Crucial to Locke's conception of personal identity is the need to exhibit my moral personhood at the Last Judgement. Locke emphasizes my conscious states as making up my personhood, insofar as these are what I may be held accountable for in relation to the laws of faith and reason. Furthermore Locke argues that this "personhood" is distinct from my body and from my soul, to allow that God may choose to give me a new perfect body at the Day of Judgement, and also to allow that my personhood can be held accountable, and is stable, whether or not the soul is ultimately immortal.[16] On this day God will revivify my forgotten memories, so that I can present myself as a conscious moral whole before Judge and Lawgiver.

Now what gives me my identity here? In Spinoza's case there seemed to be little relation between my "moral personhood" and my identity as such, insofar as I was ultimately individuated in relation to that of me which was eternal. This eternal part had nothing to do with my mortal limits, with any way I know myself as a finite being.

Locke's case seems to be diametrically opposed, although equally disastrous. Moral personhood is the central concept that individuates me and unifies me. Even my continuity is to be understood as one responsible mortal being capable of being judged. This is beyond, and opposed to, my substantial nature, my existence as soul or body. It is what I have appropriated to myself in this world, via my actions and my will, to make myself capable of judgment. But if the limits of my mortality bear a necessary relation to the grant of immortality, and if my reconstituted moral personhood is really what I am, then the issue of personal identity is fraught with the same difficulties we saw with regard to the independent rational status of the law. What holds me together is an external agency, whose purpose may be rational, but who is by definition beyond the ken of human reason.

Therefore, the centrality of immortality as a promise and a goal in Locke's philosophy adds up to an untidy picture. We have the three different categories of the epitaph: my self with my virtues and vices, only of interest to me and my Savior; the rational truths I have discovered and promulgated which are rationally appropriated to me; and this and many other crumbling tablets. It seems that the three hover untidily around immortality, the goal toward which spirits strive, that "new and higher principle of a Spiritual life," my perfected and rational state. That is only granted to those who are worthy. It is both me (if I am so worthy) and not me; it is both the central fact of this world, and not.

V. CONCLUSION

For Spinoza the consequence of my eternity was that my immersion in this world of morals and politics no longer formed part of my ultimate identity. This did not mean that there were no morals or politics, or that they were not deducible and rationally comprehensible. Although they were something I engaged with, they were also largely cast away. This was the consequence of replacing my continued immortal existence, the vulgar promise of the theologians, with eternity. With immortality gone, the bearing of this finite state on me went with it.

For Locke, preserving immortality within a rational philosophy is split between my understanding of my identity and God's understanding; and God's is a precondition of the grant of immortality. I can only know myself finitely and weakly, the full self that I must take responsibility for. The self that may not result in immortality escapes me. Immortality as such escapes me! It is always beyond my finite limits and the finite limits of my reason. Trying to explain it in terms of a natural conception of morality and reason, the concept is always beyond our reach. It is no wonder that Locke has so little to say about a naturally deduced morality, other than that it exists.

It would seem appropriate to conclude by pointing toward possible responses to this dichotomy: Kant's conception of a rational religion and strong theory of personal identity that attempts to explain moral obligation without recourse to voluntarism; or Hume's theory of the social self which can explain how our virtues and vices are shared with, and constituted by, others, and can have an existence independent of my particular appropriated character. But neither makes so stark as Spinoza what sort of commitment the commitment to eternity is. And although we may be uneasy about seeing our finitude as dross, this does not mean it is *not* dross. And no one makes so clear as Locke the lure of immortality, the starkness and interconnectedness of life and death, and their mutual bearing on our moral lives and selves—that this tablet will both perish and speak volumes.

NOTES

Thanks to Alfredo Ferrarin for his helpful response, to Knud Haakonssen for his helpful suggestions, and to Lee Rouner and Barbara Darling-Smith for the invitation to give the paper, their comments, and not least their hospitality.

    1. Maurice Cranston, *John Locke: A Biography* (London: Longmans, 1957), p. 482.

    2. Victor Nuovo, ed., *John Locke and Christianity: Contemporary Responses to the Reasonableness of Christianity* (Bristol: Thoemmes Press, 1997), p. 47.

    3. John Locke, Appendix 5: "Spirit, Soul, and Body," in *A Paraphrase and Notes on the Epistles of St. Paul to the Galatians, 1 and 2 Corinthians, Romans, Ephesians*, ed. Arthur W. Wainwright, 2 vols.(Oxford: Clarendon Press, 1987), 2:676–77. Locke does not distinguish "immortality" and "eternity" with great consistency, but seems to prefer "immortality." Locke is also suspicious of "eternity," noting that "everlasting" often does not mean "eternal" (as in "everlasting torment"). See Locke, Appendix 6, "Resurrectio et quae sequuntur," in *A Paraphrase*, p. 681.

    4. I will refer to all quotations from Spinoza's *Ethics* by the numbers of the propositions (hence Book 4, Proposition 67 of the *Ethics* will be rendered "4.67"). All translations are my own, and are made from *Spinoza Opera*, ed. Carl Gebhardt, 5 vols. (Heidelberg: Carl Winters Universitätsbuchhandlung, 1972; originally published 1925).

    5. Ibid., 1.8.

    6. Ibid., 5.41.

    7. Ibid., 5.41S.

    8. Ibid., 4.64.

    9. Ibid., 5.41S.

    10. Ibid., 5.33–36.

11. See, for example, John Locke, *The Reasonableness of Christianity as Delivered in the Scriptures*, intro. Victor Nuovo (Bristol: Thoemmes, 1997; reprint of the 1794 edition included in Locke's *Works*), p. 140.

12. Ibid., pp. 150–51.

13. See, particularly, Locke, *A Paraphrase*, 2:501–2n26 and *Reasonableness*, p.142.

14. When characterizing the difference between pagan and Christian morality, Locke excuses the former on the grounds that "they were under no obligation; the opinion of this or that philosopher was of no authority" (Locke, *Reasonableness*, p. 141).

15. John Locke, *An Essay Concerning Human Understanding*, ed. Peter Nidditch (Oxford: Clarendon Press, 1975), 2:xxi.

16. See Locke, "Resurrectio et quae sequuntur."

Metaphorical Immortality:
Some Platonic Reflections

DAVID L. ROOCHNIK

Mortal nature always seeks, as far as possible, to be immortal. In one way only can it do this: by generation. For with this it can always leave behind something new in place of the old. Only for a while can each one of the living things be called alive and to be the same, as a man is said to be the same from childhood until he becomes old. This man, however, despite being called the same, never possesses the same things in himself. He is continually becoming new, while in other ways also being destroyed. Some things he loses, like his hair, his flesh, his bones, his blood, and his body altogether. And not only his body, but also in the ways of his soul—his habits, opinions, desires, pleasures, pains, fears—each of these is never present in the same fashion, but some come into being while others are destroyed. And much stranger is this, that even when it comes to things we know, some come to be while others are destroyed in us. Never are we the same when it comes to knowledge, for what we know suffers the same fate. What we call studying implies that our knowledge is departing; for since forgetfulness is the departure of knowledge, while studying implants new knowledge in place of that which departs, it preserves our knowledge such that it seems to be the same.

Every mortal thing is preserved in this way; not by keeping it exactly the same forever, like the divine, but by replacing what goes off or gets old with something which is fresh but like it. Through this device, Socrates, a mortal being participates in immortality both in its body and everything else. By no other means can it be done. (Plato *Symposium* 207d–208b)[1]

155

So speaks Socrates, who, he claims, is recounting the words of his teacher, the priestess Diotima. The passage thoroughly articulates what I will call "metaphorical immortality." This means that human beings are not in fact, or literally, immortal. There is, however, a "device" (*mêchanê*) that allows us to "participate" in immortality, although not really. The "device" is *genesis*, generation, bringing something into being which remains (for a while) after we are gone. Through this alone do we partake, however metaphorically, in immortality.

The primary instance of metaphorical immortality is, of course, sexual reproduction. Like the other animals and the plants, human beings long to leave something of themselves behind in the form of offspring. But there are other ways of fulfilling such longing, for there are metaphorical instances of pregnancy and childbirth as well. Indeed, earlier Diotima had described "all human beings" as "pregnant" (206c) in order to account, via this metaphor, for human activity in general. The politician's pursuit of fame, the wife's self-sacrifice, the work of the poet and the craftsman (208c–209a) are examples. Ultimately, the most adequate "device" for attaining metaphorical immortality is the "generation of beautiful speeches (*logoi*)" (210b). Rational activity, for this is what *logoi* means in this context, provides human beings with a glimpse of, and therefore allows them to participate in, the eternal form of "beauty itself with respect to itself" (211b). Philosophy, the attempt to articulate the nature of such forms, is the most satisfying version of human striving.

This view of metaphorical immortality assumes that human beings are radically finite. Because we are aware of our finitude, we desire to go beyond it. Since we cannot literally do so, we engage in acts of generation to propel some vestige of ourselves into a future we will not occupy. In short, metaphorical immortality implies we are *essentially* temporal. Consciousness of, and a response to, the flow of time makes us who we are. As Diotima proclaimed in the long passage with which I began, everything slips away: our hair, our flesh, our bones, as well as our knowledge. It is in how we respond to this overwhelming fact that we become who we are. We either become students "studying" hard to retain what little knowledge we have, or athletes working out to prevent the body from getting too soft. We have children, or we make money or art. We make laws, or we pursue fame. Anything to keep going.

Other animal species engage in sexual reproduction as a means of attaining metaphorical immortality, but attaining it by metaphorical means is the province of human beings alone. To reiterate, for Diotima, to be human is to respond to the flow of time by attempting to transcend it, all the while knowing this cannot really be done.

Plato's most penetrating analysis of the temporality of human experience comes, I think, in Socrates' account of the "negativity" of Eros, which can be translated here as both "desire" and "love" and which is the subject of the *Symposium*. If someone loves, Socrates argues, that someone loves something, some X (199d). If someone loves X, he lacks and does *not* have X (200b). There is an obvious counterexample: it seems possible for someone to love some X which he already has. We can, for example, love health while being healthy. Socrates responds: if someone desires X, and already has X, then what he really wants is for "what is now present to be present in the future" (200d). What is loved/desired is "that which is not available to someone and which he does not have," and furthermore to have this absent object "preserved and . . . present into the future" (200d).

Human desire is negative: we want what we *don't* have. Human being is essentially temporal, and time negates: what we do have we won't have soon. Since it is necessarily temporal, and therefore implicated in a continual series of negations, human experience is not self-sufficient. It can never be positive, never be in and of itself. As a result, the ultimate object of human desire, as Diotima will later argue, is to possess what we want not just into the future, but for "always" (*aei:* 205a7). This leads to her most extravagant claim: the true object of eros, of human striving itself, is not children or art or fame or money. It "is immortality" (207a).

The view just sketched fuels Diotima's description of metaphorical immortality. Whether one finds it compelling or not, two items in it should at least be surprising. First, Plato puts this description of radical finitude and the consequent striving for metaphorical immortality into the mouth of a priestess (201d), who one might expect to hold a more enduring, more substantial, less temporal, conception of the soul. Second, regardless of what character speaks these lines, they were written by Plato, widely known as the first and perhaps the foremost exponent of the literal immortality of the human soul. How could the author of the *Phaedo*, whose famous "arguments" for the immortality of the soul set the stage for all such future efforts in the history of Western philosophy, also write the *Symposium*?[2]

This is the main question I am exploring. To do so I will look carefully at two of the "arguments" in the *Phaedo*. I will claim that they fail. However, in failing they also succeed. They fail to prove literal immortality, but in the very act of trying to prove it, they demonstrate the truth of metaphorical immortality. To quote a poet, "my love she speaks softly/she knows there is no success like failure/and that failure is no success at all."[3]

Before commencing, a last question: are the "arguments" of the *Phaedo* simply bad ones which fall short of their stated objective, or did Plato intend the "arguments" to fail so that they might demonstrate something else? Since I find it difficult to conceive of Plato doing anything badly, I much prefer the second option. In saying this, however, I must acknowledge that I put myself into the camp of a small minority among Plato scholars, a camp whose position I cannot fully defend in a short essay.[4] Finally, however, whether (as I believe) Plato understood and even utilized the failure of his "arguments," or whether he intended them seriously and just plain botched the job, is not crucial. My real purpose is to utilize Plato, to use the "arguments" of the *Phaedo* as an occasion to explore the relationship between literal and metaphorical immortality. More specifically, I want to examine what might be described as an inversion of Pascal's wager. Recall that, for Pascal, reason cannot determine whether "God is, or He is not." Therefore, human beings must simply wager on one side or the other. But how do we decide on what side to bet? Pascal explains: "Let us weigh the gain and the loss in wagering that God is. Let us estimate these two chances. If you gain, you gain all, if you lose, you lose nothing. Wager, then, without hesitation that He is."[5] My procedure will be to hedge my bets: what happens if the "arguments" to prove literal immortality fail, as I think, and as I think Plato thinks, they do? There will still be something gained: metaphorical immortality. It won't be much. But it will be something.

In any case, on to the *Phaedo*.

Before being able to evaluate Socrates' "arguments," it is necessary first to clarify what exactly their objective is. When Socrates learns from his friends that he is going to die very soon, he seems hardly bothered at all. His friend Cebes is both perplexed and annoyed with him. He challenges Socrates: how can he face death so "easily" (62c)? To meet the challenge Socrates must justify his emotional response to death. Indeed, he must give an "apology" (63b) and defend the fact that he feels no irritation at the prospect of death. And why is this? Because, he says, "I am in good hope that there is something for the dead, and just as has been said long ago, something much better for the good than for the bad" (63c).

This statement seems to place two requirements upon the "arguments." The first is minimal and ambiguous: to show there is "something" for the dead. Second, to show there is justice, something better for the good than for the bad. The latter is the standard stuff of Plato's eschatological myths. In the *Gorgias* and the *Republic,* as well as in the *Phaedo,* Socrates tells stories of the afterlife in which the individual soul is judged and then rewarded or punished according to the justice or injustice of its actions. Such a view of justice in the next world requires the preservation of the individual soul whose moral history is retained. As Cebes soon puts it, what Socrates must show is that the soul has "power and intelligence" (70b) after it has died. Or as Socrates puts it later, in his myth, the soul takes its "education" with it to Hades (107d).

In sum, the demand apparently placed upon the "arguments" of the *Phaedo* is to prove literal, personal immortality. The individual must remain intact in order to be judged.

On to the first argument. It can be outlined as follows:

"Argument" #1

P1: If X comes to be P, and if P has an opposite, then X comes to be P from being the opposite of P (70d–e).
Examples: greater from smaller, weaker from stronger, slower from quicker, worse from the better, more just from the more unjust.

P2: Between all these pairs of opposites there are two kinds of genesis (71a).
Examples: between larger and smaller there is increase and diminution; between being asleep and being awake, there is falling asleep and waking up.

P3: Being dead is the opposite of being alive (71c).
Therefore: From the living the dead come to be and from the dead come the living. Therefore, "our souls exist in Hades" (71e).

A decisive problem with this "argument" is found in Premise #3. "Opposition" is a broad category, for within it fall both "contraries" and "contradictories." P and not-P are contradictory properties if S can't

have both but must have one. To use Aristotle's example, a whole number must be either odd or even, and it cannot be both. But this is not
the case with life and death, because it is possible for something to be
neither, namely, to be inanimate. Therefore, Socrates assumes without
justification that "opposite" means "contradictory" in Premise #3. If we
correct the premise it would then more safely read, "being not-alive
is the opposite of being alive." With this change, however, the "argument" tells us only that when we're dead, we're not alive, and when we
come into life we come from what is not-alive. It certainly proves nothing about immortality.

What, then, should the verdict be here? Even if maximum charity
is applied, and the objection just noted is suppressed, perhaps the "argument" in some sense works—that is, perhaps it does demonstrate
that the passage from death to life and back again implies that life does
not end at death. But even taken with such charity, the "argument"
hardly meets the demands Cebes had earlier placed upon it, namely,
to demonstrate that the soul retains its "power and its intelligence"
(70b) after death. Even if it does succeed in showing something about
the immortality of the species or the cosmic soul or anything else, "Argument" #1 surely fails to prove personal immortality.

Less charitably, one may simply judge the "argument" to be really bad and to prove nothing at all. Even with this harsh judgment,
however, something positive may be salvaged. Although it is deficient
as a proof of personal immortality, what Socrates has presented is
nonetheless informative. It tells us something, albeit in a very general
sense, about the nature of coming-into-being, of genesis itself. Genesis is some sort of movement between opposites. If S is P and then goes
through the process of becoming, it becomes not-P. As in the description of the temporal flow offered above, genesis is a continual sequence
of negations. Such a view was, at least, intrinsic to the pre-Socratic account of nature. As Aristotle, in describing these early thinkers, puts it,
"all conceive of opposites as basic principles."[6] My hair, formerly
brown, becomes gray; it becomes not-brown. The move between opposites—hot and cold, dry and wet, up and down—is crucial to an understanding of nature, and so opposites themselves are conceived as
basic principles of the universe.

But the analysis of genesis in terms of movement between opposites, Aristotle argues, necessarily leads to an additional principle: that
which underlies the movement. "It is clear something must underlie
the opposites, and that the opposites are always two."[7] In other words,

there must be a third basic principle. Exploring what this third principle is—matter, substratum, substance, form—would lead us not only into the heartland of Aristotelian metaphysics, but also back to the pre-Socratic search for what Anaximander called the *archê*, the "first principle," the "source," the "origin," that which underlies and thus makes possible all change.

My purpose here in mentioning Aristotle and the pre-Socratics is not to pursue their kind of theoretical explorations. Instead, it is to suggest something of the character of Socrates' first "argument": it fails to demonstrate personal immortality. Nonetheless, it accomplishes much. Most important, it presents to the mind material for philosophical reflection. Something—matter, substratum, substance, form, the *archê*—must underlie the transition between opposites. What is this "something?" Who knows? But reflection upon the oppositional nature of genesis suggests it is there. And if it is, then it is there to be sought.

If I may generalize here, the first "argument" offers a conception of being human, one akin to Diotima's account in the *Symposium*. Just as she conceived of eros, of the human soul, as "in-between" the mortal and the divine (202e)—that is, of being mortal but aspiring to the divine—so too implied in the first argument of the *Phaedo* is a sense of being human as standing in relationship to something underlying genesis, something immune to the movement between opposites. Even without, or perhaps especially without, knowing what it is, by this reflection the act of philosophical thought is vindicated. It makes sense to seek the *archê*.

The theme of movement between opposites is introduced quite early in the *Phaedo*. When Socrates is awakened by his friend Crito, his legs are painfully stiff and so he rubs them. He then says to Crito: "What men call pleasure seems so strange. For it is amazingly linked to what seems to be its opposite, namely pain, so much so that they will not both come to a man at the same time. And yet if someone pursues the one and gets it, it is virtually necessary to take the other also, as if the two were joined together in one head" (60b).

The point seems simple enough: pain and pleasure are opposites and so cannot both be present "at the same time." Furthermore, the two continually follow each other. After feeling pain, one will then feel pleasure, and vice versa. Two observations about this passage should, however, be kept in mind. First, notice how tentative Socrates' language is here. He doesn't say "pleasure"; he says "what men call pleasure." He doesn't say "the opposite of pleasure"; he says "what seems to be its opposite." He doesn't say "it is necessary that pain follow pleasure and vice versa"; he says, "it is virtually necessary."

This tentativeness can be explained by considering a second feature of this passage. By Socrates' own lights, it is simply not the case that pain necessarily follows pleasure. While pleasure may follow the suffering of pain, it is not clear the opposite is true. Indeed, in the *Republic* Socrates denies this. Smell, he says, is an example of a pleasure neither coming from nor returning to a pain.[8] Or consider the *Philebus* where the example of a "pure pleasure," one "unmixed with pain"[9] (52b), is learning.

What I am suggesting is this: early in the *Phaedo* Socrates offers a commonsensical observation. Ordinary life seems characterized by a continual flow of negations, a continual move between opposites: pain-pleasure-pain-pleasure, etc. But the tentativeness of Socrates' language in expressing this invites us to conceive of a break in the sequence, an exemption from the movement. In the case of pleasure, there are the pure pleasures of learning and smell, for they neither come from nor return to their opposites. These pure pleasures constitute, I suggest, a significant opening: it is possible for human beings to exempt themselves, not only from the pain-pleasure sequence, but from the oppositional flow of time altogether. And how do we do this? In moments of leisure, in moments of play. To explain both what I mean and why I'm not really digressing as badly as it seems, I turn to another passage in the *Phaedo*.

Socrates is discussing the life of the philosopher, which he describes as a kind of "purification" (67c). By this he means that because philosophers devote themselves to the life of the mind (or the soul), they degrade the importance of their bodies. Indeed, the body is a distraction or an impediment to the working of the mind, which philosophers try to overcome. For my purpose, what is most striking is the way Socrates describes this, the worst feature of the body: "For the body, on account of its need for sustenance, deprives us of leisure in a myriad of ways" (66c). The summary charge against the body is that it causes *ascholia* (66c), the lack of leisure. The importance of leisure is signaled in the prologue of the *Phaedo*. Echechrates asks Phaedo to tell the story of Socrates' death, if, that is, Phaedo is not lacking in leisure (*ascholia*: 58d). Phaedo agrees by saying, "I have leisure (*scholazô*: 58d).

In moments of leisure, unconstrained by the exigencies of the clock, the demands of authority, the madness of politics and money, the desires of the body, or the expectations of others, we are free. Free to do what? To play. In the act of play, as thinkers such as Huizinga and Pieper have explained, we look neither to the future in anxiety nor to the past in regret.[10] We are absorbed in a particular, self-enclosed space at a particular, self-contained moment. We are immersed in the present. In this sense, play releases us from the flow of time.

Recall that in the *Philebus* learning is counted as a pure pleasure. Recall also that the etymology of "school," the place of learning, is in *scholê*, leisure, and the connections will now be clear. Real learning requires leisure, as Aristotle says about "mathematics" (whose etymology is in *manthanein*, "to learn").[11] The Egyptian priests were the first to engage in this sort of purely theoretical endeavor because "they had leisure" (*scholazein*). Only in moments of leisure can pure pleasure in the form of philosophical reflection, philosophical play, be attained. Only then can "[the philosopher] using pure thinking itself by itself attempt to hunt down each of the beings purely itself by itself" (*Phaedo* 66a). Only then can thinking try to become pure enough to think objects immune to the flux of time.

To summarize this line of thought: Socrates offers an "argument" for the immortality of the soul. It fails. But it succeeds in challenging, in presenting possibilities for thought. Reflection on the nature of genesis, the movement between opposites, sparks the question whether something exists beyond, and immune to, the oppositional flux of time itself. Indeed, reflection on the continual negations of time—here today, gone tomorrow—does just this as well. As suggested in the first discussion of the *Symposium*, temporal experience cannot make positive sense of itself. Looking into time means looking through a window for something not in time. What this something is, or whether it even exists, is not clear. But it doesn't matter. What does matter is that there is good reason for us to philosophize, to ask whether this something exists, and if it does what it might be; to ask whether this question itself matters. There is good reason to wonder about our temporal existence. In doing so, we achieve, however precariously, metaphorical immortality. If the "argument" to prove literal immortality fails, it also, in this sense, succeeds.

It should now be clear why, throughout this essay, I have placed "argument" in scare quotes whenever I used it to describe what Plato is doing in the *Phaedo*. Although Plato inspired centuries of attempts to prove the literal immortality of the soul, it is not obvious that he himself actually argues for this proposition. Instead, to revert to the language I've been developing above, he "challenges," "suggests," "provokes," "presents" questions for reflection. In doing so, he provides material for, and thereby justifies, the life of philosophy. He achieves metaphorical immortality.

On to the second "argument."

"Argument" #2

P1: The equal itself is something (74a).

P2: We know the equal itself (74b).

P3: Sensed equals, e.g., sticks and stones, seem "sometimes equal to one, but not to another" (74b).

P4: Equals themselves never seem unequal (74c).

P5: Therefore, sensed equals are not the same as the equal itself; sensed equals fall short of the equal itself (74d).

P6: Sensed equals remind us of the equal itself (74d–e).

P7: We could not derive knowledge of the equal itself from sense-experience.

P8: Knowledge of the equal itself is *prior* to sense-experience.

P9: Sense-experience begins at birth (75b).

Therefore, knowledge of the equal itself was acquired *prior* to birth (75c). Therefore, "our souls did exist earlier, before entering human form, apart from bodies, and they possessed wisdom" (76c).

What does this "argument" actually accomplish? As Cebes immediately notices (77c), even if successful in proving the prenatal existence of the soul, it would hardly demonstrate the soul's survival of death, which is the crucial requirement of the "argument." But does it even prove prenatal existence? Not really.

The equality, in length, of sticks or stones is available to human judgment only through the presence of the equal itself, in comparison to which the equality of sticks or stones "falls short." In other words, since any pair of equal sensible objects must also, in some sense, be unequal, when one judges that, for example, "these two sticks are equal" (in, say, length), appeal is made and access is available to an equality which never exhibits inequality. This, the "equal itself," must (somehow) originate in a source other than the sensible experience. In short, the condition of the possibility for a judgment about sensible equality is some sort of *a priori* knowledge of the equal itself.

What I have just said is barely a sketch, and its elaboration would generate controversies of all kinds. Not least of these is this question, on which Plato scholars are much divided: What exactly does it mean to say that sensible items "fall short" of the equal itself? For my purpose, the key is only this: we are aware of the inadequacies of sensible experience. When we say, "these two sticks are equal in length," we know they are not exactly equal, or that even if they are, they will be unequal when compared to a third stick. And yet, even into the ordinary inadequacies of everyday life a hint of formal perfection regularly intrudes. For we do say, even if we don't quite know what we mean, "these two sticks are simply equal." Even more powerfully (from Plato's point of view), we can count such sensible items. I am holding two sticks. "Two," unlike the sticks, will always be exactly "two." And so questions are prompted: What in the world is "two" anyway? Where does it come from? Where in the world did we get this altogether unexpected "concept" of equality?

The examples just cited are mathematical in nature. They involve counting or measurement. This is no accident, since, for Plato, mathematics is the most illuminating beacon in our intellectual lives. In the language of the *Republic*, the ordinary act of counting "turns us around," from becoming and sensible experience, to being and the possibility of an intelligible realm.[12] Counting, numbers, the equal itself, introduce some measure of formal perfection, of intelligible and extraordinary stability, into our ordinary lives. As such, to use the language of the *Theaetetus*,[13] they cause the philosopher to "wonder." To wonder about what? How can there be stability in the midst of flux? How can, to use the specific example of the *Theaetetus*, six dice be both greater than four and less than twelve? On the one hand, this is an easy question to answer: by remaining the same when being compared first to a larger number and then to a smaller one. On the other hand, this is no easy question at all, for it naturally prompts reflection on the nature of number itself. Even more difficult is this question when applied to human being itself. Socrates intimates just this sort of difficulty when he asks (in an echo of Diotima's teaching), How it is that "I, who do not, at my age, either increase in size or diminish, am in the course of a year first larger than you, who are young, and afterwards smaller, when nothing has been taken from my size but you have grown?"[14] How is it that I stay the same while all the time changing? Do "I," in fact, really stay the same at all?

In sum, reflection upon the ordinary acts of counting and measuring generates questions about the origin, the grounding, of the stable intelligibility present in our daily lives. In the asking of these questions, we become philosophical.

To summarize again: Plato's second major "argument" for the actual immortality of the soul fails. But it also succeeds. By sparking the search for the meaning and origin of "the equal itself," by calling it "recollection," it instantiates the quest for metaphorical immortality.

In order to explain further why I regularly put "argument" into scare quotes, allow me a comparison. Recall that Augustine, in all earnestness, uses just this sort of Platonic strategy to argue, without the scare quotes, for the immortality of the soul. For example, he says this: "For if there persists anything in the mind unchangeable, which cannot exist without life, then life must also remain in the mind eternally. For indeed the mind is so constituted that if the antecedent is true, the consequent is true. Moreover, the antecedent is true. For who dares say . . . that the principle (*ratio*) of number is changeable?"[15] In other words, because the soul thinks about numbers, or simply counts, and because numbers are unchanging and eternal, so too must the soul be. This proof, which appears in a variety of permutations throughout Augustine's writings, takes its bearing from the mind's ability to cognize non-sensible items. As such, it is a clear legacy of Platonism. But it is not necessarily equivalent to what Plato himself is doing. For there are so many holes or openings in Socrates' "arguments" that, as I have been arguing, one must either judge them to fail in their objective of proving personal immortality, or one must invoke the scare quotes and try to explain what other value these "arguments" could have.

For another contrast, consider this equally "Platonic" statement by Thomas Aquinas: "Everything naturally aspires to being after its own manner. . . . The senses indeed do not know being, except under the conditions of here and now, whereas the intellect apprehends being absolutely, and for all time; so that everything that has an intellect naturally desires always to exist. But a natural desire cannot be in vain. Therefore every intellectual substance is incorruptible."[16]

Simply to assert my view, it is not at all clear that Plato believes "a natural desire cannot be in vain." In other words, like Augustine and Aquinas, not to mention Aristotle, Plato is profoundly impressed by the mind's ability to think non-sensible items such as "the equal itself" or numbers or universals. For the Christian philosophers, this fact becomes important evidence of personal immortality. A similar judgment, or interpretation, cannot safely be made about Plato's *Phaedo*.

The third "argument" roughly goes like this: there are two kinds of substance, the composite and the incomposite. It is probably the case that the composite both changes, and then disperses or dies, while the incomposite neither disperses nor dies. The soul, in thinking items like the equal itself, is far more akin to the incomposite. Therefore, like the incomposite, it does not disperse or die.

There are additional steps and nuances to this "argument." Simply note the conclusion: "the soul is most like the divine and immortal and intellectual and uniform and indissoluble and ever unchanging" (80b). I think it is obvious that this argument is not conclusive. Even if the soul is somehow like the entities which it thinks, and even if it thinks some entities are changeless, this does not imply that the soul is changeless. Indeed, if the soul becomes similar to what it thinks, it itself must go through a great many changes, since the soul thinks different kinds of objects. To reinvoke the primary requirement of these "arguments," it certainly does not prove that the individual soul, with its moral history preserved, remains intact after death.

Space does not permit me to explore the details any further than this. Nor will it allow me to discuss the fourth "argument," which in fact is the most complicated of them all. I simply outline it for your perusal.

Argument #4

P1: The opposite itself will never be opposite to itself (103c). Example: heat/cold.

P2: Heat is something different from fire, and cold is something different from snow (103d).

P3: Snow will never admit heat; fire will never admit the cold (103d).

P4: "Not only is the form itself entitled to its own name for all time, but there's something else too, which is not the same as the form, but which, whenever it exists, always has the shape of that form" (103e).

Reformulation: "It's not only opposites themselves that don't admit each other. This is also true of all things which, although not opposites to each other, always have the opposites" (104b).

Example: The "odd" must always have this name. Three is "odd," but is not the same as the odd. Just like odd, three can't be even.

Example: Fire does not admit cold.

P5: The proper cause of a thing's being P must itself be P and must be incapable of being -P.

P6: The opposite of life is death (105d).
P7: The soul is the proper cause of being alive (105c).
Therefore, the soul will never admit death (105e).

All sorts of issues, especially relating to the word "cause," need to be treated at length. Space permits me only one observation. The theme of opposites once again dominates this "argument." Indeed, to invoke the mythological reference to Theseus with which the dialogue opens (58a), I would claim that opposites function like "Ariadne's thread" to lead us through the maze of complexities making up the *Phaedo*. Without rehearsing any of the details, I simply assert that this final "argument" aims to push thinking beyond (behind, beneath, above) the continual flux of oppositional negation to the pure positivity of what is immune. The scare quotes used to describe what Socrates does are therefore appropriate. The goal here is not to cement a conclusion, but to provoke philosophical thought.

To conclude: In the *Poetics* Aristotle says, "Metaphor is the application of an alien name by transference either from genus to species, or from species to genus, or from species to species, or by analogy." To cite an example Aristotle uses in the *Rhetoric*, when Homer describes the Trojan spears which missed their targets, he says, they "stood fast in the ground, though they longed to take their full of flesh."[17] The spears "are given a sort of life and purpose of their own; they *want* to sink into the flesh of the enemy."[18] A characteristic of one species, the human, is transferred to another, the inanimate tool. A spear, after all, cannot want. A metaphor, then, is a linguistic "device" used to cross boundaries, to bring features of one kind into another. As Christopher Ricks once put it, "whatever else a metaphor may be, it is a relation."[19]

To talk about the immortality of the human soul is to transfer what really belongs to the divine to the human. On the one hand, such talk is not literally true. It is, however, more than "merely" metaphorical. It is, to use a peculiar phrase, metaphorically true. By this I mean that talk about immortality captures something true about being human. Just as a metaphor crosses boundaries, so too do we. We are essentially relational beings. We are, as Diotima in the *Symposium* puts it in her description of Eros, "a great spirit (*daimôn*)," living precariously "between the divine and the mortal" (202e). To be human, as Plato both argues and regularly shows, is to seek to move beyond the negative flow of time, to seek for what is positive, and present, stable and always there even when we are not. To be human is thus to be metaphorical, to live in-between, in the attempt to become something we can never be.

All of this is, I believe, demonstrated by Socrates' "arguments" to prove the immortality of the soul. They fail. But their failure is like success, even if it is no success at all.

NOTES

1. Plato *Symposium* 207d–208b. I follow, but make significant changes in, the translation of W. Lamb (Cambridge: Harvard University Press, 1975). The Greek text I use is Burnet.

2. I. M. Crombie is forthright in his response to this dilemma: "This passage from the *Symposium* is either to be explained away or regarded as unique; it should not cause us to modify the account we have given of Plato's main doctrine of the soul" (*An Examination of Plato's Doctrines* [New York: Humanities Press, 1962], p. 363).

3. Bob Dylan, "Love Minus Zero/No Limit," from *Bringing It All Back Home*, 1965. Thanks to Professor Alfredo Ferrarin, who I hope is right in reminding me of the source of this wonderful line.

4. For a view similar to my own, see Peter Ahrensdorf, *The Death of Socrates and the Life of Philosophy: An Interpretation of the Phaedo* (Albany: State University of New York Press, 1995).

5. Pascal *Les Pensees* 81.

6. Aristotle *Physics* 1.5.

7. Aristotle *Physics* 1.7.

8. Plato *Republic* 584a–b.

9. Plato *Philebus* 52b.

10. Johan Huizinga, *Homo Ludens* (Boston: Beacon Press, 1955); Joseph Pieper, *Leisure: The Basis of Culture* (New York: Pantheon, 1962).

11. Aristotle *Metaphysics* 1.1.16.

12. Plato *Republic* 521c–525b.

13. Plato *Theaetetus* 155b–d.

14. Plato *Theaetetus* 155b.

15. Augustine *On the Immortality of the Soul*, chap. 5.

16. Aquinas *Summa Theologica* 1.75.6

17. Homer *Iliad* 11.574; cited in Aristotle *Rhetoric* 3.11.3.

18. M. M. Wilcock, *The Iliad of Homer* (London: MacMillan, 1978), p. 306.

19. Christopher Ricks, "In Pursuit of Metaphor;" in *What's Happened to the Humanities*, ed. A. Kernan (Princeton, N.J.: Princeton University Press, 1997), p. 182.

The Meanings of Life

DAVID SCHMIDTZ

APOLOGY

I remember being a child, wondering where I would be—wondering *who* I would be—when the year 2000 arrived. I hoped I would live that long. I hoped I would be in reasonable health. I would not have guessed I would have a white-collar job, or that I would live in the United States, or that the new millennium would find me speaking to audiences about the meaning of life. But that is life, unfolding as it does, meaning whatever it means. I am grateful to be here. I also am simply amazed.

I am forty-four. Not old, but old enough that if I die today, it is as likely to be from a heart attack as from a car accident. Old enough that friends and family are beginning to provide more occasions for funerals than for weddings. Old enough to love life for what it is. Old enough to see that it has meaning, even while seeing that it has less than I might wish.

I am an analytic philosopher. Analytic philosophers are trained to spot weaknesses in arguments. Unfortunately, that sort of training does not prepare us for questions about life's meaning. A perfect argument, Robert Nozick suggests in jest, would leave readers with no choice but to agree with the conclusion.[1] When we think about life's meaning, though, we are not trying to win a debate. Success in grappling with the question is less like articulating and defending a position and more like growing up.[2] Perhaps that is why academics have written so little on the meaning of life, despite its being arguably the central topic of philosophy. (As a vague indication of how intimidating a topic this is, consider that the September 1999 *Philosophers Index* on CD-ROM lists only 102 entries under the topic of "meaning of life" since 1940. By way of comparison, the Index lists 3,339 works under the topic of "justice.") Speaking to analytic philosophers about life's meaning is like stepping into a boxing ring in search of a dance partner. Or so we fear.

Perhaps there is no excuse for venturing into an area where we cannot meet our usual standards. More likely, one way of respecting philosophical standards is by not trying to apply them when they are not apt, thus refusing to let them become a straitjacket—a caricature of intellectual rigor. So, I do not here seek the kind of argumentative closure that we normally think of as the hallmark of success in analytic philosophy. This essay is simply an invitation to reflect. I try to get closer to some real (even if inarticulate) sense of life's meaning by reflecting on what it has been like to live one.

Questions about life's meaning often are synonymous with questions about its value—but not always. By analogy, if the subject were an abstract painting, its meaning and its value would be different (though probably related) topics. Likewise, when we wonder about life's meaning, the question sometimes is less about what makes life good and more about what makes life significant—what purpose is served by living it. We may even feel a need for such purpose to be granted to us by some outside agency. But if Iris Murdoch is correct, "there are properly many patterns and purposes within life, but there is no general and as it were externally guaranteed pattern or purpose of the kind for which philosophers and theologians used to search. We are what we seem to be, transient mortal creatures subject to necessity and chance."[3]

WHAT THE SAGE KNEW ABOUT THE LIMITS OF MEANING

Introducing the question of life's meaning in *Philosophical Explanations*, Nozick says the question is so important to us, and leaves us feeling so vulnerable, that

we camouflage our vulnerability with jokes about seeking for the meaning or purpose of life: A person travels for many days to the Himalayas to seek the word of an Indian holy man meditating in an isolated cave. Tired from his journey, but eager and expectant that his quest is about to reach fulfillment, he asks the sage, "What is the meaning of life?" After a long pause, the sage opens his eyes and says, "Life is a fountain." "What do you mean life is a fountain?" barks the questioner. "I have just traveled thousands of miles to hear your words, and all you have to tell me is that? That's ridiculous." The sage then looks up from the floor of the cave and says, "You mean it's not a fountain?" In a variant of the story, he replies, "So it's not a fountain."[4]

The sage feels none of the angst that led the seeker to the cave. So, who's missing something: sage or seeker? The story suggests a contrast of attitudes. I'll call them Existentialist and Zen, meaning only to gesture at the traditions these names evoke. The Existentialist attitude is that life's meaning, or lack thereof, is of momentous import. We want meaning. If we don't get it, we choose between Stoicism and despair. The Zen attitude is that meaning isn't something to be sought. Meaning comes to us, or not. If it comes, we accept it. If not, we accept that too. To some degree, we choose how much meaning we need. Perhaps the sage achieves peace by learning not to need meaning. Perhaps that's what we're meant to learn from the sage's seemingly meaningless remark that life is a fountain.

The Existentialist insight, in part, is that meaning is something we give to life. We do not find meaning so much as throw ourselves at it. The Zen insight, in part, is that worrying about meaning may itself make life less meaningful than it might have been. Part of the virtue of the Zen attitude lies in learning to not need to be busy: learning there is joy and meaning and peace in simply being mindful, not needing to change or be changed. Let the moment mean what it will.

Nozick concludes the section with another story.

A man goes to India, consults a sage in a cave and asks him the meaning of life. In three sentences, the sage tells him, the man thanks him and leaves. There are several variants of this story also: In the first, the man lives meaningfully ever after; in the second he makes the sentences public so that everyone then knows the meaning of life; in the third, he sets the sentences to rock music, making his fortune and enabling everyone to whistle the meaning of life; and in the fourth variant, his plane crashes as he is flying off from his meeting with the sage. In the fifth version, the person listening to me tell this story eagerly asks what sentences the sage spoke. And in the sixth version, I tell him.[5]

Another joke? What are we meant to imagine happening next? What does Nozick the fictional character say? Nozick the author never tells us, unless we read the book's final seventy pages as Nozick's effort to imagine what we might extract from the sage's three sentences. My theory is, the fictional Nozick should say, "Naturally, the sage said life is a fountain. Why? What did you expect?"

Expecting the story's punch line to be a life-changing revelation would be comical. The punch line has to be comical because the whole story—climbing a mountain to ask a sage for a dazzling revelation—is comical from the start. The thing to expect from a sage is sagacity, not revelation. The message in the sage's cryptic answer is that the seeker has to figure it out for himself. There isn't much anyone else can tell him. The fulfillment we are seeking when we ask about life's meaning cannot be handed to us in the form of a jingle.

It would not be comical if the seeker asked not for the meaning of life but for the meaning of *his* life. What specifically makes *his* life meaningful?[6] That question does not invite the "life is a fountain" reply. It invites reflection on what it is like, or would be like, to have lived that particular life. To that question, the sage might respond that, for the seeker, meaning comes from time he spends with his family rather than time he spends at the office.[7] Or, a true sage might tell the seeker that if he finds meaning when he goes back to his suburban life, it will be because he creates it there—not simply in virtue of what he chooses but also in virtue of how he attends to what he chooses—and no lifestyle ensures he will successfully undertake such creation.

I have achieved the age of mid-life crisis, an age when many become rich enough to worry less about money and more about mortality. Although I have no sense of crisis, I still need to make an adjustment, for the struggle of youth is over and something else is taking its place. When I was fifteen, the game was to figure out what I could do with my life that I would be proud of thirty years later. Today, the game somehow is not about the future anymore. It feels as if the world has grown still, as if time is slowing down, and now the point is no longer to prove myself and make my place in the world but to understand the place I've made, respect the meanings it can have, and just live. Perhaps I feel different because my father died last year. I do not expect ever to rebound fully from my father's death, but on the other hand, I feel no need to rebound fully. My family and friends will go on without me some day, or I will go on without them. My wife will go on without me, or I without her, and while that knowledge saddens me, it also makes me grateful for today.

I no longer identify with the seeker. I now feel empathy for the sage. Having been asked to explain the meaning of life, I want to say, "I should know?" Yet, here I am, having agreed to write on this topic. So, I must think of something, knowing that if I try too hard to find the answer that will mark me as a true sage, I will look less like a sage and more like a person who is trying too hard to look like a sage.

LIMITS

There is such a thing as limited meaning. Some lives mean more than others, but the most meaningful lives are nonetheless limited in their meaning. Consider some of the ways in which life's meaning might be limited. First, meanings need not last. A life or a part of life may have a meaning that truly matters but that nevertheless does not matter forever. A life's meaning might boil down to the meaning it had at a particular time. A life's meaning could be manifest relatively early in life and then be over. We might say a particular episode or a particular stage had enduring meaning even while allowing that other episodes or stages meant little or nothing. Or we might say a particular episode—getting the highest grade in high school calculus—truly had meaning, but the meaning did not last. We might accurately say, "It meant a lot at the time." Why would that not be enough? *When* would that not be enough?

Second, meanings change. Even when meaning lasts a lifetime, it is not constant. Short though life may be, it lasts long enough for its meaning to evolve. Life meant one thing on my first date and something else on my twenty-fifth wedding anniversary. To look for meaning that does not change is to look, I suspect, for something that is at best purely formal, and at worst a mirage.

Third, meanings need not be deep. As some people use the word, a meaning is deep when it leaves no question unanswered, no longing unfulfilled. If that is what people are longing for when they long for deep meaning, what should they do? Some longings are best handled by getting over them rather than by trying to fulfill them, and this may be an example. Perhaps we should not think of meaning as a deep phenomenon. I do not know.

Or if deep meaning is possible, maybe life per se is not the kind of thing that can have it. Life is a cosmic accident. It is not here for a purpose. It is simply here, and that is all there is to it. A deeply worthwhile life is simply a series of mostly worthwhile—sometimes deeply worthwhile—episodes. Life as a type of thing is not meaningful. In a sense, neither are individual lives per se (life-tokens, as philosophers might say). Instead, an individual life is simply an allowance of time. Meaning resides in how we spend it. We might wish we had more to spend, but meaning emerges from how we spend, not how much we spend.

Fourth and finally, life is short. Would life mean more if it lasted longer? Quite possibly. On the other hand, if life truly lacked meaning, making it longer would not help. Nozick asks, "If life were to go on forever, would there then be no problem about its meaning?"[8] There would still be a problem, as Richard Taylor shows in his recounting of the myth of Sisyphus.[9] Sisyphus was condemned by the gods to live forever, spending each day pushing the same stone to the top of the same hill only to see it roll back down to the bottom. The life is paradigmatically pointless, and no less so in virtue of lasting forever.

Unlike Sisyphus, of course, we are mortal. We achieve immortality of a kind by having children to carry on after we die, but Taylor says that only makes things worse. Life still "resembles one of Sisyphus' climbs to the summit of his hill, and each day of it one of his steps; the difference is that whereas Sisyphus himself returns to push the stone up again, we leave this to our children."[10] Having children is as pointless as anything if all we accomplish is to pass the same dreary struggle—the same rock of Sisyphus—down through generations.

Ultimately, any impact we have is ephemeral. "Our achievements, even though they are often beautiful, are mostly bubbles; and those that do last, like the sand-swept pyramids, soon become mere curiosities, while around them the rest of Mankind continues its perpetual toting of rocks."[11] And if we had a lasting impact? So what? As Woody Allen quips, what he wants is immortality not in the sense of having a lasting impact but rather in the sense of not dying.

So, death and the prospect of death can limit how much a life can mean. Yet, limiting life's meaning is a long way from making it altogether meaningless. As Kurt Baier observes, "If life can be worthwhile at all, then it can be so even though it is short. . . . It may be sad that we have to leave this beautiful world, but it is only so if and because it is beautiful. And it is no less beautiful for coming to an end."[12] Moreover, if looming death can affect us in ways that make life mean less, it also can affect us in ways that make life mean more, at least on a per diem basis, for if we are going to die, time becomes precious. People who know they are terminally ill often seem to live more meaningfully. Though dying, they somehow are more alive. They cherish each morning, and are vividly aware of each day's passing. They see despair as a self-indulgent waste, and they have no time to waste.

I do not know why we are not all like that. I suppose something changes when the doctor actually delivers the prognosis. Our daily schedules are the result of an ongoing war between what is truly important and what is merely urgent, and the latter normally wins. Even rudimentary self-preservation often is lost in the daily blur. Before my brother was diagnosed with lung cancer, a part of him was gripped by a fantasy that the world would give fair warning: the day would come when a doctor would see a small lump on an X-ray, and Jim would have to quit smoking that very day or else the lump would turn out to be terminal cancer. Jim did quit that very day, too, but the lump was not a warning.

Commentators have treated Taylor's article as a definitive philosophical counsel of despair regarding life's meaning, but near the end of the article, Taylor offers a lovely counterpoint that seems to have gone unnoticed. Taylor says people's lives do resemble that of Sisyphus, and yet, "The things to which they bent their backs day after day, realizing one by one their ephemeral plans, were precisely the things in which their wills were deeply involved, precisely the things in which their interests lay, and there was no need then to ask questions. There is no more need of them now—the day was sufficient to itself, and so was the life."[13]

Perhaps therein lies an idea that is as close as we reasonably can come to specifying the nature of a life's meanings. There is more than one sense in which even a short life can have meaning, but for people's lives to have meaning in the sense that concerns us most is for people's wills to be fully engaged in activities that make up their lives. One way in which our lives engage us, that is not threatened by life's brevity, is by virtue of fitting into a larger design. But perhaps that is not really the sort of meaning we want. The life of a cow on a factory farm has that sort of meaning. Accordingly, Existentialist and Zen attitudes both presuppose that a life's meaning cannot derive entirely from how it fits into a larger plan. The Existentialist attitude is that the plan must be of our own devising, and must be one in which we play an active role. The Zen attitude is that no plan is needed. The Zen way involves learning not to take the separateness of persons too seriously, thus learning there is no deep self that has or needs to have any particular meaning in the grand scheme of things.

Taylor observes, "On a country road one sometimes comes upon the ruined hulks of a house and once extensive buildings, all in collapse and spread over with weeds. A curious eye can in imagination reconstruct from what is left a once warm and thriving life, filled with purpose. . . . Every small piece of junk fills the mind with what once, not long ago, was utterly real, with children's voices, plans made, and enterprises embarked upon."[14]

Where did those families go? Day after day, they bent their backs to the building of lives that appear as mere bubbles in retrospect. Yet, as Taylor goes on to say, it would be no "salvation to the birds who span the globe every year, back and forth, to have a home made for them in a cage with plenty of food and protection, so that they would not have to migrate any more. It would be their condemnation, for it is the doing that counts for them, and not what they hope to win by it. Flying these prodigious distances, never ending, is what it is in their veins to do . . ."[15] The point of human life likewise is to do what it is in our veins to do, knowing we have choices that migratory birds do not. The special glory of being human is precisely that we have such choices. The special sadness lies in knowing there is a limit to how right our choices can be, and a limit to how much the rightness of our choices can matter.

MEDITATIONS ON MEANING

There is something wrong with lists. Lists are boring. They fail to make us stop and think. They fail to illuminate underlying structure. With misgivings, then, this section lists things that tend to go with living a meaningful life. None is a necessary condition of meaningful life; there need be no particular feature that all meaningful lives share.

There probably is no such thing as the very essence of meaning. Different lives exhibit different features, and the features I discuss need not be compatible. At the same time, even features that are in some sense contraries may come together to endow a life with meanings, for a life is not a logically pristine sort of thing. To give a simple example, some things mean what they mean to me partly because of the price I paid for them. Other things mean what they do partly because they are gifts.

The first feature I will mention, though, does seem just about essential, namely that meaningful lives, in one way or another, have an impact. Most crucially, the counsel of despair typically is grounded in an observation that our lives are not of cosmic importance. Therein lies the beginning of a fundamental error. The question is not whether I can identify something (such as the cosmos) on which my life has no discernible impact. The question is whether there is anything (such as my family) on which my life *does* have a discernible impact. The counsel of despair typically is grounded in a determination to find some arena in which nothing is happening and to generalize from that to a conclusion that nothing is happening anywhere. This fundamental error seems ubiquitous in the more pessimistic contributions to the literature on life's meaning.

There are innumerable impacts our lives could have but do not, and there is nothing very interesting about that. It makes no sense to stipulate that a particular impact is the kind we need to have so as to be living a meaningful life, when other kinds of impact are on their own terms worth having. If we wish to find meaning, we should look, not where the impact isn't, but where the impact is. Life's meaning, when it has one, is going to be as big as life, but it cannot be much bigger than that. It will not be of cosmic scope.

Nozick says, "A significant life is, in some sense, permanent; it makes a permanent difference to the world—it leaves traces."[16] I wonder why. Why must the traces we leave be permanent? More generally, is it possible to try too hard to leave traces? One thing you notice about philosophers, at least the productive ones, is that hunger for leaving traces. It must be a good thing, that hunger. It makes people productive, and in producing, they leave traces. And yet, the hunger is insatiable so far as I can tell. No amount of attention is enough. We all know the kind of person—many of us *are* the kind of person—who gets anxious because our reputations do not match Robert Nozick's. (The few who attain that stature go on to fret about Bertrand Russell.)

And so just as surely as there is something good about the hunger to leave traces, there is something bad too. Even while that hunger fuels our efforts to leave valuable traces, it leads us to overlook the value of the impermanent traces we actually leave.

Here are some of the other features meanings can have. Again, think of these as independent meditations. As I was writing, I had to make a choice, and it seemed more important simply to express the thought, not letting it be twisted by an overarching goal of making different thoughts fit neatly together.

1. MEANINGS ARE SYMBOLIC: Taylor recalls his experience seeing glow worms in New Zealand. There are caves "whose walls and ceilings are covered with soft light. As one gazes in wonder in the stillness of these caves it seems that the Creator has reproduced there in microcosm the heavens themselves, until one scarcely remembers the enclosing presence of the walls. As one looks more closely, however, the scene is explained. Each dot of light identifies an ugly worm, whose luminous tail is meant to attract insects from the surrounding darkness."[17] The worms are carnivorous, even cannibalistic. To Taylor, it epitomizes pointlessness.

I was intrigued when I read this because, by coincidence, my wife and I have been to New Zealand's Glow Worm Grotto. I cherish the memory. We got up at 4:00 in the morning so we could get there before the sun came up. We got there in time, and we were the only ones there. The cliff wraps around in a horseshoe and the walls nearly meet overhead, creating the impression of being in a cave. We knew what we were looking at, but still they were a beautiful sight—hundreds of glowing blue dots all around us, alive! Of course we find no meaning in the bare phenomenon. That's not how meaning works. Meaning is what the phenomenon symbolizes to a viewer. Elizabeth and I were there to celebrate our lives together, and celebration it was. That we could be in New Zealand at all, that we could get up long before dawn to see something together, unlike anything we had ever seen before, and that we could be together, alone, in this grotto, thoroughly and peacefully in love, sharing this silent spectacle of glowing blue life, blown away once again by the thought of the wonders we've seen together—that's meaning. No one needed glow worms to be intrinsically meaningful, any more than ink on a page needs intrinsic meaning to be meaningful to readers. No one needed glow worm life to be meaningful to glow worms, not even glow worms themselves. That was never the point.

The point was, we were capable of attributing meaning to them and to their home and to our fleeting chance to share it with them.

But perhaps you would have had to be there, or at least have had similar experiences, to understand. That too is meaning. Meaning isn't some measurable quantity. There is something perspectival and contextual and symbolic about it. Taylor and I could be standing in the same place seeing the same phenomenon and the experience could be meaningful to me but not to him. That's how it works.

Had I been there by myself rather than with Elizabeth, I would have seen the same thing but it would have meant so much less. The experience meant what it did partly because I shared it with her. The day was sufficient to itself, partly because it was a symbolic microcosm of a sufficient life, but neither the day nor the life would have been sufficient without her.

2. MEANINGS TRACK RELATIONSHIPS: Meaning ordinarily is not solipsistic. Typically, when our lives have value to the people around us, they come to mean something to us as well, in virtue of meaning something to others. Our lives become intrinsically valuable to us by becoming intrinsically valuable to others.

Our lives also become intrinsically valuable to us by becoming *instrumentally* valuable to others. A few years ago, I joined thousands of others in trying to save a small community in Kansas from rising floodwaters, as we surrounded it with dikes made of sandbags. We failed. Had we known our efforts would have no instrumental value, it would have been pointless to proceed as we did. But so long as we thought we might succeed, the effort had an intrinsic value predicated on its hoped-for instrumental value. The effort meant something—it made a statement—because of what we were trying to accomplish.

The idea that meaning tracks the making of statements suggests we might be able to connect the rather metaphorical idea of life's meaning to meaning in a more literal sense. When we talk about meanings of words, we normally are talking about how they function in an act of communication. Maybe life's meaning likewise is tied to what it communicates, to themes people read into it. A further thought: Not all communication is intentional. Even if there's nothing we intend our life to symbolize—no statement we intend our life to make—it still can mean something, communicate something, to other people. Life might have meaning of a kind without our knowing about it.

3. MEANINGS AS GIFTS: Nozick says, "Love of life is our fullest response to being alive, our fullest way of exploring what it is to be alive."[18] Our reward for loving life is to have a number of good years, lovable years. If that is not reward enough, then the flaw is less in the nature of the reward than in the nature of the love. It is the ultimate case of looking a gift horse in the mouth, and the fault is in us, not in the gift. The fault lies in our not loving life for what it is. We should be properly aware of what comes to us. We should be properly grateful for what comes to us, and properly cautious about insisting we need more.

Meaning also can emerge from an exchange of gifts. If my life means something to people around me, then it means something, period. What if their lives are not meaningful, though? Don't their lives need to have meaning before their lives can have the power to confer meaning on ours? If so, are we not looking at an infinite regress?

No. Not at all. We need not get the meanings of *words* from something bigger than us. Nor must we look to something bigger for meaning in our lives. We get it partly from communion with each other, just as we get the meanings of words. Meaning can be our gift to each other. Or it may sometimes be a consequence of living in a way that does justice to the gift. We need not seek meaning in some source outside the relationship. Even if our lives have meaning only because of what we mean to each other, that is still something. Limited meaning is real meaning. It is the kind of meaning lives can have.

4. MEANINGS AS CHOICES: Life's meaning is contingent on how we live. As life takes one direction rather than another, so does its meaning. Meaningfulness is not guaranteed. Life is not obliged to meet expectations. It need not answer to our preconceptions. Does life have enough meaning? Enough for what? No fact of the matter determines whether the meaning a life has is enough. We decide. Is it worth striving to make our lives mean as much as it turns out lives can mean? We decide. Is it worth getting what is there to be gotten? We decide.

What is a person? Among other things, persons are beings who can choose to see their experiences as meaningful. By extension, persons can choose to see their *lives* (or other lives) as meaningful. The less inspiring corollary is, persons also can choose to see their experiences, and by extension their lives, and other lives, as meaningless. We all choose for ourselves whether to exercise this capacity. If we do exercise it, though, we are making a mistake. An optimist would say, if it is meaningless, then so is being hung up about its meaninglessness. We may as well enjoy it.

An incurable pessimist might say that misses the point, because it is not possible to enjoy that which is pointless. But a Zen optimist rightly could respond: That's not quite true. Closer to the truth: we can't enjoy what we *insist* on *seeing* as pointless. Part of what makes life meaningful is that we are able to treat it as meaningful. We are able and willing, if all goes well, to make that Existentialist leap. (Or we simply let it be meaningful, which would be a sort of Zen leap.)

Singer John Cougar Mellencamp once titled a record album, "Nothin' matters, and what if it did?"—a humorous title, humorous because we see the paradox. Someone who was sufficiently pessimistic would not. Having acknowledged that something matters, the pessimist is the one who would fail to appreciate the paradox in going on to say, "So what?"

5. MEANINGS TRACK ACTIVITY: The Experience Machine, described in Nozick's *Anarchy, State, and Utopia*, lets us plug our brains into a computer programmed to make us think we are living whatever we take to be the best possible life. The life we think we are living is nothing but a computer-induced dream, but we do not know that.[19] Whatever would be part of the best possible life for us (the optimal mix of wins and losses and adversities triumphantly overcome—anything at all) will in fact be part of our felt experience. "Would you plug in? What else can matter to us, other than how our lives feel from the inside?"[20] Most people say they would not plug in, even though by hypothesis their felt experience would be as good as felt experience can be.

The lesson is that when we have all we want in terms of felt experience, we may not yet have all we want. Something is missing, and it seems fair to describe the missing something as life's meaning. Meaning is missing because activity is missing. Meaning resides not exactly or solely in what happens to us. Meaning tracks activity—not how we *feel* about activity, but activity per se. Closely related: Meaning tracks accomplishment, not how we feel about accomplishment. As Nozick puts it, "we want to do certain things, and not just have the experience of doing them."[21] Mere felt experience isn't enough to confer meaningfulness. Nozick says we also want to be a certain kind of person, and "there is no answer to the question of what a person is like who has long been in the tank. Is he courageous, kind, intelligent, witty, loving? It's not merely that it's difficult to tell; there is no way he is."[22]

Meaning may also track something related to activity, namely the making of contact with an external reality. Several years ago, my sister visited me in Tucson. I took her to the Sonoran Desert Museum just outside Tucson. At the museum is a cave. As we descended into the cave, my sister marveled at how beautiful it was. After a few minutes, though, her eyes became accustomed to the dark. She took a closer look, and reached out to touch the wall. "It isn't real. It's just concrete," she said, deflated.

Why was she disappointed? Because she thought the cave was a magically wild "other" when in fact it was an Experience Machine. If what we experience is a human artifact, intended to produce a certain experience rather than being some independent miracle of nature, that somehow cheapens the experience, at least in some contexts. Maybe the problem with the Experience Machine is not only that the experience it provides is a mere dream. It is also a dream deliberately scripted. In failing to connect us to a wild "other," it also fails to make us more real, and thus fails to give life meaning.

If you go to zoos, you have probably witnessed little kids ignoring the tigers and zebras and squealing with excitement about a ground squirrel running down the path beside them. The kids know: the squirrel is real in a way zoo animals are not. Somehow, there is more meaning in the wild—in experiences that have not been scripted, especially by someone else.

Even if I am correct in saying meaning tracks accomplishment as such, it may remain that the *feeling* of meaningfulness tracks the *feeling* of accomplishment, which still leaves us with a version of the question posed by the Experience Machine. Do we want our lives truly to have meaning, or would the feeling of meaningfulness be enough? Here is a disturbing thought: the feeling of accomplishment often seems to fade over time. Does the fading diminish only the feeling of meaningfulness, or does it also diminish the meaningfulness per se?

MEANING AS A PERSONAL TOUCH

Nozick finds it "a puzzle how so many people, including intellectuals and academics, devote enormous energy to work in which nothing of themselves or their important goals shines forth, not even in the way their work is presented. If they were struck down, their children upon growing up and examining their work would never know why they had done it, would never know *who* it was that did it."[23]

Life is a house. Meaning is what you do to make it a home. Giving life meaning is like interior decorating. It is possible to overdo it, so that the walls become too "busy." But if our walls are bare, the solution is not to stare at bare walls, or philosophize about their meaning, but to put up a few photographs, making the walls reflect what we do, or care about, or making them reflect our judgment about what is beautiful or worth remembering. Activity can be meaningful, and philosophical reflection can be meaningful activity if done in the right way and if kept in its place—if we take it seriously without taking it too seriously or taking it seriously in the wrong way. We need not be afraid of bare walls or deceive ourselves about their bareness. Neither is there any reason to dwell on the "fundamental underlying" bareness of walls we have filled with pictures. If we do that, we are not being deep. We are pig-headedly ignoring the fact that the walls are *not bare*. We are failing to take our pictures seriously, which is metaphorically to say we are failing to take seriously what we do with our lives. We are saying, what would be the meaning of this life (the wall) if the activities that make it up (the pictures) were not real? But they *are* real.

There are questions we are not good at answering. Or maybe we are not good at accepting answers for what they are. We do what we do. It means what it means. Thomas Nagel says, "Justifications come to an end when we are content to have them end. . . . What seems to us to confer meaning, justification, significance, does so in virtue of the fact that we need no more reasons after a certain point."[24] After a point, further questions betray something like the willful incomprehension of a child who has no purpose in mind to help her see when it is time to stop asking "Why?" Meaning resides in what we do, what we care about, what we or others judge to be beautiful or worth remembering about life—not the wall but the pictures that adorn it over the years.

METAMORPHOSIS

Nozick's *The Examined Life* begins with an observation that we fly through life on a trajectory mostly determined before we reached adulthood. With only minor adjustments, we are directed by a picture of life formed in adolescence or young adulthood.[25] Nozick concludes that book by wondering what the fifteen-year-old Nozick would think of the person he grew up to become.[26] Interesting question. Why might we want an answer? Consider what Nozick says in an earlier book. "The young live in each of the futures open to them. The poignancy of growing older does not lie in one's particular path being less satisfying or good than it promised earlier to be—the path may turn out to be all one thought. It lies in traveling only one (or two, or three) of those paths."[27]

I think I understand. Every day, doors click shut behind us, on paths we might have taken, on meanings life might have had. No matter. The Zen insight, in part, is that meaning emerges not from picking the right door so much as from paying attention—the right kind of attention—to whatever path we happen to be on. If this life is to mean what we want it to mean, it will happen as a result of attending to the path life actually takes, not dwelling on what might have been, or even on what might yet be.

Maybe it is easier for me, because the paths I envisioned when I was young were all pretty grim compared to the path I ended up on. In one of the possible worlds closest to this one, the end of the millennium finds me delivering mail in Prince Albert, Saskatchewan. The turning point in this actual world occurred almost exactly twenty years ago, when I had been a full-time mailman for nearly five years, and as I was waiting for the Post Office to transfer me from Calgary to Prince Albert. While I was waiting, I signed up for a night school course on Hume's *Treatise*. I took it because it was the only course that fit my schedule. By the time the transfer came through, I knew I could no longer be a mailman. Had the transfer come through earlier, or had that time slot been occupied by some other course, then as far as I know I would still be a mailman today. I am fairly sure I would not have gone to night school; Prince Albert had no university.

Being a mailman was my "dream job" as I was growing up. It was not a bad life. The only nightmarish thing about that possible world is that, from time to time, that version of me would have woken up in the middle of the night to the realization that there comes a time to be a seeker, not a sage, a moment not for Zen acquiescence but for hurling oneself at an unknown future. The Zen way is partly an appreciation of the danger in wanting too much, but this world's mailman saw, just in time, what a terrible thing it can be to want too little. Had I not learned that lesson when I did, I would have let the moment pass, growing old mourning for a world that might have been, trying to love life for what it is, but not fully succeeding. So, when I contemplate versions of me that might have been, versions quite a bit more probable than the me who actually came to be, I feel a kind of weak-in-the-knees gratitude and relief: it so easily could have been me. For nearly five years, it *was* me. Yet, through a series of miracles, I now find myself in that barely possible world where the mailman gets invited to give a paper on the meaning of life.

On some philosophical topics, we reflect so as to reach a conclusion. On this topic, the reflection itself is the objective. There is no proposition we can write on a blackboard that would count as stating the meaning of life. The point of the exercise is not to articulate a proposition but to mull things over—the relations and activities and choices that make up a particular life. The point of reflection is to have a feel for the meaning in your own life, and contact comes from the process, not from reaching conclusions. So an essay like this can never be more than work in progress.

One of the best things I ever did was to coach little league flag football. But if I had to explain how something so mundane could mean so much, I would not know where to begin. I could have told my players they were accidents of natural selection in a quite possibly godless world, but that bit of information was not germane to our shared task of living that part of our lives to the hilt. Year after year, four years altogether, we had a mission, my players and me, a mission that left no void needing to be filled by talk of meaning. On the contrary, life was, however fleetingly, a riot of meaning. It was as Taylor says. There was no need to ask questions. There is no need now. The day was sufficient to itself, and so was the life.

NOTES

This paper originally was written for presentation at the Boston University Institute for Philosophy and Religion in December 1999, and for publication in *Robert Nozick*, ed. David Schmidtz (New York: Cambridge University Press, 2001). We gratefully acknowledge Cambridge University Press's permission to use it here. I thank the University of Arizona, the Social Philosophy and Policy Center at Bowling Green State University, and the Centre for Applied Ethics at the University of British Columbia for supporting my research. Thanks also to Carrie-Ann Biondi, Pamela J. Brett, Dan Dahlstrom, Peter Danielson, Walter Glannon, Wayne Norman, Lee Rouner, Paul Russell, Kyle Swan, and Teresa Yu for generous and thoughtful reflections on the topic. And I thank Elizabeth Willott, not so much for the paper as for the life that enabled me to write it.

1. Robert Nozick, *Philosophical Explanations* (Cambridge, Mass.: Harvard University Press, 1981), p. 4.

2. In Nozick's words, "Give us specific problems to solve or paradoxes to resolve, sharp questions with enough angle or spin, an elaborate intellectual structure to move within or modify, and we can sharply etch a theory. . . . However, thinking about life is more like mulling it over, and the more complete understanding this brings does not feel like crossing a finishing line while still managing to hold onto the baton; it feels like growing up more." See Robert Nozick, *The Examined Life: Philosophical Meditations* (New York: Simon and Schuster, 1989), p. 12.

3. Iris Murdoch, *The Sovereignty of Good* (New York: Routledge and Kegan Paul, 1970), p. 79.

4. Nozick, *Philosophical Explanations*, p. 571.

5. Ibid., pp. 573i–74.

6. I thank Wayne Norman for this insight.

7. Nozick wonders (in *Philosophical Explanations*, p. 572) whether this is what we think the seeker expects to hear.

8. Ibid., p. 579.

9. Richard Taylor, "The Meaning of Life," in *The Meaning of Life*, ed. E. D. Klemke, 2d ed. (New York: Oxford University Press, 1999), pp. 167–75.

10. Ibid., p. 172.

11. Ibid.

12. Kurt Baier, "The Meaning of Life," in *The Meaning of Life*, ed. Steven Sanders and David Cheney (Englewood Cliffs, N.J.: Prentice-Hall, 1980), p. 61.

13. Taylor, "Meaning of Life," p. 174.

14. Ibid., p. 172.

15. Ibid., p. 174.

16. Nozick, *Philosophical Explanations*, p. 582.

17. Taylor, "Meaning of Life," p. 170.

18. Nozick, *Examined Life*, p. 301.

19. Robert Nozick, *Anarchy, State, and Utopia*, (New York: Basic Books, 1974), pp. 42–45.

20. Ibid., p. 43.

21. Ibid.

22. Ibid.

23. Nozick, *Philosophical Explanations*, p. 578.

24. Thomas Nagel, "The Absurd," *Journal of Philosophy* 68 (1971): 716–27, reprinted in Klemke, *Meaning of Life,* p. 180.

25. Nozick, *Examined Life*, p. 11.

26. Ibid., p. 303.

27. Nozick, *Philosophical Explanations*, p. 596.

Author Index

Subject Index